Problems and Prospects of Public Debt Management and its Impact of Social and Human Development

(with special reference to Manipur)

Problems and Prospects of Public Debt Management and its Impact of Social and Human Development

(with special reference to Manipur)

Dr. Aribam Devidas Sharma

Sunmarg Publishers & Distributors
H.No. 36, Maidan Garhi, New Basti,
Post IGNOU, New Delhi-110068

Sunmarg Publishers & Distributors
H.No. 36, Maidan Garhi, New Basti,
Post IGNOU, New Delhi-110068
Mob: +91-9718986843, 9717502501
Email: sunmargpublishers@gmail.com

Branches: New Delhi • Manipur • Imphal

Problems and Prospects of Public Debt Management and its Impact of Social and Human Development

ISBN : 978-93-82606-86-4
1st Edition : 2022
Price : ₹ 850/-
Paper 80 gsm sunshine

Published by Mohit Tiwary for M/s. Sunmarg Publishers & Distributors, New Delhi-110068

PRINTED IN INDIA

Dedicated

To My Elder Brother

(L) Aribam Deveswar Sharma

PREFACE

Among pressing problems of backward states in India, indebtedness undoubtedly occupies the first place. In many respects, the debt problems of the backward states like Manipur are financial reflection of the more deeply rooted inconsistencies of the development process, which are generating imbalances on an even larger scale and deepening the gap between the north-eastern states and the rest of the states. Since the constituent states of the Indian Union are highly heterogeneous in terms of economic size, there is a need for state-specific assessment of debt sustainability status. This is the reason why debt problem n state like Manipur needs in-depth specific study.

The issue of containing public debt at sustainable level has been a major concern at the level of both centre and states and management of the debt crisis will be the central issue in the 21st century. While the financial crisis of the union government has so far been averted, there is little sign that the burden of debt servicing faced by many states has become less burdensome, indeed for many debtor states the situation has been deteriorating. The problems arising from the growth of public debt of the state governments in particular has not been seriously examined. The severity of debt problems faced by any states suggests a continuing need for new approach at the state level. No doubt the RBI has made study of the growth and debt sustainability at state levels without venturing into any in-depth analytical investigation for states specific. However, the RBI as the banker and debt manager to the state government has repeatedly stressed (in its Annual Reports and other publications), the need to address the underlying issues relating to debt sustainability. Even the related problems states' unauthorized overdraft from the RBI had been separately investigated by successive Finance commissions It is surprising to note that, the consequential problem arising out of growth of states specific government indebtedness to the union government has not given its due attention either by the RBI or state governments or even the economist. The present study makes an attempt to fill up this gap. The study covers the period from 1980-81 to 2005-06,however, the study covers the period from 1972 to 73 ,wherever necessary as it deals with the post statehood period and wherever possible the period of the study brought up-to-date by reference to the latest materials.

Against this backdrop, the objective of the present study is to examine and assess the debt problems of the state as well as to look into whether public debt management has been effective in achieving a positive impact on social and human development in the state.

The secondary data on which reliance has been placed are: Finance Accounts, Govt. of Manipur, CAG reports, The Reserve bank of India Publications: Bulletins, Annual Reports, Occasional Papers- various issues, Public Finance, Govt. of India and other related journals and books were used for the study.

The present study is divided into seventh chapters. The first chapters studies, background of public debt, the need for the study of public debt to the states, the reason for mounting Public debt in the states' constitutional framework of intergovernmental borrowing in India and some issues of new borrowing regimes. The second chapter deals with definition of Public debt, magnitude and composition of debt of the states, classification o loans and repayments.

Chapter three examines the reasons for sharp deterioration in the states finances, genesis of fiscal crisis in Manipur, public debt management, problems and prospects, roles and objective of public debt management. Chapter four examines some issues in the controversy of the concept of the public debt and its impact on revenue and capital budgets of Manipur, debt burden on economic development. Chapter five examines social sector, relationship between economic development and human development, human development and economic growth, pubic debt management and its impact on social development by using UNDP methodology.

Chapter six studies the state's debt and finance commissions.

Chapter seven summarizes the studies made in the earlier chapters. So, policy recommendations are also suggested which may be helpful to manage state's debt effectively.

ACKNOWLEDGEMENT

It is my great pleasure to acknowledge many persons who have directly and indirectly helped me in the completion of this work. First of all, I would like to express my deep respect and gratefulness to my thesis supervisor, Prof. Amar Yumnam for introducing me in the Public Economics and encouraging me to tackle difficult problems independently from the very beginning of research work. It was because of a great deal of independence provided by him that I could gain a very good experience in diverse topics. Without his constant encouragement and help at many critical times, this work could not have been possible, from which I could bring in this book form. I would also like to acknowledge the encouragements and supports I have received from all other faculty members and non-teaching staff of the Department of Economics, Manipur College and Manipur University. It will be plainly seen to what extent I am indebted to the work of other scholars and I wish to make a frank and grateful acknowledgement to all those from whose work, I have freely quoted. I cannot thank enough all my friends, Tangkeswor, and Ibomcha. I also thank Librarian and Staff of Manipur University, Rattan Tata memorial Library, Delhi School of Economics, JNU Library, New Delhi, NIPFP, New Delhi.

Dated: Aribam Devidas Sharma

Place: Imphal

LIST OF TABLES

Table No.	Heading	Page No.
2.1	Outstanding Debts of States Governments	35
2.2	Composition of Outstanding Liabilities of state Governments	36
2.3	Debt/GDP ratio and Annual Growth of Debt of State Governments	38
2.4	Outstanding Debt of Government of Manipur	40
2.5	Outstanding Debt of Manipur Government (in percentage form)	41
2.6	Amount of gross and net Loans taken by the Government of Manipur	44
2.7	Compositions of Central Loans to the Government of Manipur	47
2.8	Composition of Plan and Non-Plan Loan in Total Loan	49
2.9	Plans Loans taken by the Government of Manipur	52
2.10	Non-Plan loans taken by the Government of Manipur	53

2.11	Debt/NSDP data of Government of Manipur	55
3.1	Fiscal Health of the State Manipur	61
3.2	Transfer of Resources from the Centre to the State of Manipur	63
3.3	Distribution of states on the basis of debt as percentage of GSDP (in 19998-99 and 2002-03)	75
3.4	Debt profile and effective Rates of interest	79
3.5	Growth of interest payment: Centre and States	80
3.6	Interest Rate category-wise Distribution of outstanding market Loans for the Year 2002-03, 2003-04 and 2006-07	83
3.7	Internal loans taken by the Government of Manipur	84
3.8	Limits of WMA	87
3.9	Ways and Means Advances to Government of Manipur	89
3.10	The extent to which Manipur maintained the required minimum balances with the RBI	92
3.11	Average utilization of normal WMA and overdrafts by State governments	93
4.1	Financial Burden of Central Loans on the Revenue Budget of Manipur (Crores)	104
4.2	The financial burden of union Loans on the state (Interest charges on Union Loans as percent of states tax revenue, Total Revenue and state Revenue Expenditure) of Manipur	106

4.3	The financial burden of Union loans on the Capital Budget of the state, Manipur (in crores of rupees)	110
4.4	Financial burden of Union Loans on the Budget of the Manipur (Interest and Repayment of Union Loans as percent of total tax revenue total revenue and total revenue expenditure of the state)	111
4.5	Financial Burden of internal debt of Manipur	113
4.6	Outstanding debt as percentage of NSDP of Manipur	114
4.7	Economic Development impact Central Loans on the Manipur	116
4.8	Comparative studies of the rate of growth of Central Loans and NSDP of Manipur	119
4.9	Burden of debt repayment and servicing to the state's aggregate expenditure (revenue + capital)	121
5.1	Select Social Sector Expenditure Ratios	138
5.2	A Composition of public spending in India- Some critical Ratios for 1990-91 and 1998-99	141
6.1	Debt forgiveness by Finance Commissions	152
6.2	Debt redemption scheme	158

CONTENTS

Preface *vii*

Acknowledgement *xi*

List of Tables *xiii*

1. Introduction 1
2. Magnitude, Composition and Trends in the Public Debt of Manipur 26
3. Debt Crisis: An Overview on Debt crisis; An Evaluation of causes 58
4. Burden of Public Debt 99
5. Social Development Impact of Public Debt Management 124
6. Finance Commission and State's Debt 144
7. Conclusion, Major Findings and Policy Recommendations 164

Bibliography 193

CHAPTER 1

INTRODUCTION

The debt problem at the State level has been a major problem in federal financial relations and is of direct concerns to the indebted states. Union loans to the states have loomed large in the total federal financial transfers such as grants and tax shares. Union Loans involve a reverse flow of financial transfers in the form of payment of interest and repayment of principal in India. Thus, the issue of containing public debt at sustainable level has been a major concern at the level of both centre and states. While the financial crisis of the union government has so far been averted, there is little sign that the burden of debt servicing faced by many states has become less burdensome, indeed for many debtor states the situation has been deteriorating. Public authorities are no doubt realizing the economic implications of the problems created by growth of state's indebtedness. These problems have roused the interests of the economists as is evident from some studies made on public debt of states.

Overview of Literature on Public Debt

The spate of problems of public debt in recent years have grown stimulus to new ideas and concepts in the analysis of

Public debt both in theoretical and practical aspects. Most of the analysis in economic literature of the growth and role of public debt has been conducted in terms of situation obtaining in economically developed countries of west. Hence, we begin by exploring previous literature on Public Debt relating to developed countries.

The development of this literature can be portrayed chronologically by referring to some selected works, even though many authors have contributed to the literature. Lerner (1948) advanced the thesis that the burden of the debt rests upon people at the time the debt is created, as illustrated by the aphorism "we owe it to ourselves".

In sharp contrast, Buchanan (1958) argued that public debt allowed people in the present to shift the cost of government onto people in the future. Barro (1974) denied the ability of public debt to transfer cost forward in time because, with inter-generational altruism, an increase in debt would be accompanied by an increase in saving to pay the future taxes required to service the debt. And in another paper, by the same author published in 1979, discussed the "Ricardian" equivalence theorem on public debt i.e. the proposition shifts between debt and tax finance for given amount of public expenditure would have no first-order effect on the real interest rate, volume of private investment, etc. Aiyagari and McGratten (1998) concluded that the welfare gains or losses of variations in debt are small. This is due in large part to their choice of the utilitarian welfare criterion in combination with the specific level of transfers assumed. A study by Martin Floden has shown that even if changes in government debt have little impact on utilitarian welfare measure, the insurance value of increasing debt can be large.

The implications of the paper by Jaime De Pinies is that if additional finance were forthcoming, imports could be larger while still keeping debt-to-export ratios on a declining trend. So long as debt-to-export ratios are on a declining trend, the debtor country is solvent and will be able to repay its debt.

A study by Paul Krugmanhas presented a highly abstract analysis of the issues involved in dealing with the developing country debt problems. He has argued that the best way to think about debt problems is as one of the debt that overhang, the inherited debt of some countries is larger than that of the present value of the resource transfer than their creditors expect them to make in the future. The paper by Alessandro Prati studies an episode of hyper-inflation that took place in France in the mid 1920s and suggests that a long and balanced maturity structure would increase a government's ability to resist a run on a government debt. Guillermo A. Calvo's study highlighted that expectations may play a crucial role in the determination of equilibrium when the government debt is auctioned off to the public, and there is no attempt to manage expectations or to peg interest rates. Joao Victor issler, Luiz Renato lima presents tests on the sustainability of Brazillian public debt for the post war period 1947-1992. They show that debt is sustainable only if seigniorage is included as a government revenue.

Given the overview of literature on public Debt, a new survey on debt analysis is needed for updating the recent development on debt analysis. The works of Avramovie (1964), King (1968) and Solomon (1977) can be mentioned here. Assuming a target growth rate, in conjunction with a fixed capital output ratio and fixed marginal propensity to save, Solomon shows that debt/output ratio will be bounded if target rate of growth is greater than real interest rate. Kharas (1984) looks at a situation in which government borrowing from abroad for infrastructural facilities where the returns go to the private sectors. If the government is constrained in its ability to raise tax rate, the expansion of tax base is required for debt servicing.

In line with the above overview of literature on Public Debt and Debt analysis, it becomes more relevant to do a similar survey of literature of Public debt at state level. Although there is an extensive literature on Public debt Financing and debt analysis, there has been little research on the study at state level. Therefore, we need to have a fresh survey of literature relating to my study. We begin by exploring previous literature confining to India only. Seshan. A (1987) was the first to draw a pointed attention to the possibility of domestic debt in India reaching an unacceptably high level in the none too distant future. Subsequently, the Report of the Controller and Auditor General (CAG) of India (1988) also warned against the alarming growth in domestic debt.

The initial studies, based on simple trend analysis, were criticized by Rangarajan, Basu and Jadhav, on the grounds that they lacked 'analytical constructs' behind the findings. This study called for a comprehensive and much deeper analysis on measurement of budget deficit and debt. In their pioneering work the authors examined the dynamic nexus between the two. Using data for the 1970s and 1980s, the authors simulated two alternative scenarios for financing the deficit: a debt financing scenario and a monetary-financing scenario.

Under the debt-financing scenario, they concluded that "the higher interest burden may invariably lead to a squeeze on budgetary capital outlays, thereby stifling economic growth". Under the monetary-financing scenario they concluded that "resorting to monetary financing is likely to set in motion a vicious circle of large deficit, higher monetary financing, greater inflation leading again to a larger deficit".

H. D. Pathak (2001) outlines econometric models for the Indian Economy to study dynamic inter-relationship between domestic public Debt management conducted by RBI and Fiscal operations of the Government. While assessing the debt sustainability for the state governments, Prasad, Goyal and Prakash (2003) discussed that the outstanding debt of the state governments would touch 34 percent in 2007-08 from the level of 26 percent in 2002-03.

Another work by Goyal, Jeevan and Ray[18] (2004) which assesses the inter-temporal budget constraint using co-integration techniques observes that government finances are unsustainable both at the central and the state levels, though there is some signs of weak sustainability, if combined finances are considered. Recognizing that unsustainable public debt is likely to have a major adverse impact on monetary policy objectives, financial stability and public debt management, the Reserve Bank of India (RBI) in successive Annual Reports since 1991 has been advocating fiscal prudence. The research conducted in the Department of Economic Analysis and Policy (DEAP), and published in the Report on Currency and Finance (RCF), particularly, for the years 1998-99, 2000-01 and 2001-02, has highlighted the issues relating to sustainability of public debt and deficit. The thrust of this analysis was to set out a methodology, to assess sustainability and to recommend policy for achieving fiscal prudence.

The RBI Annual Reports for 2000-01 and 2001-02 recommend durable fiscal consolidation through revenue maximization. Another recent work by Reserve Bank of India (RBI) has made a study of Debt Sustainability at state level in India (August 2005), which addressed the issue of debt sustainability in India at state-level, if at all, only at an aggregate level across all states, or at an even higher level of aggregation including the Centre. The study noted that, "Studies on debt sustainability in the Indian context have tended to be confined to the Central Government, or to state finances only at a consolidated level. State-wise analysis is conspicuous by its absence."

G. Thimaiah's, Burden of Union Loans on the States (1977), is a study which tried to analyze the problems of Union loans to the states in the Indian federation within the framework of modern theory of fiscal federalism, and suggested certain short term and long term solutions to reduce the financial and economic burden of the union loans on the states. Central Loans to States under Five Year Plans (1991) by Tapan Kumar

Shandilya, made a detailed exhaustive study and analysis of magnitude, direction and impact of central loans to states under five year plans specially after fourth five year plan. However, the study was made with special reference to Bihar state only.

Need for the Study of Public Debt of the Specific State

It is quite relevant to quote here what T.Shandiyla said, "loan financing has occupied a very important place as a method of resource mobilization to finance economic development in a modern state". It is now used as a means to stimulate economic development and achieve the wider objective of economic planning.

The Eighth Finance commission took that "There is nothing basically wrong in the growth of public debt". With the expanding public functions, no government particularly in a developing economy, can undertake large scale programs of development without recourse to borrowing. The Sarkaria

Commission in its "Report on Centre-State Relations" has agreed with the observation of the Commission.

The Eighth Finance commission took the stand, "The centre has to view States requirement in perspective of total needs". The development of the country as a whole is a collective responsibility of the centre and state governments.

For the purpose of development, the central government territory includes all the states". The Eighth Finance commission also views, "The growing volume of central assistance for the plan is an indication of the partnership between the union and states in the coming the hands of the governments in order to pursue their economic growth-oriented policy and also to promote the social welfare o the society".

This has led the states blaming the Union government's policy providing plan assistance to the state's plan mostly in loans and with unjustifiable terms and conditions to these loans. In a way, this problem ha created a sense of dissatisfaction among the states. Even, the related problems of state's unauthorized overdrafts from the Reserve Bank of India (RBI) were separately investigated and policy measures were suggested by the Fifth Finance commission which has minimized the seriousness of the problem indebtedness. But the consequential problem arising out of the growth of state governments' indebtedness to the union government has not been given its due attention either the RBI or by the state governments or even by the economists. It is only the union government which drew the attention of the central government and therefore finance commissions have been asked for finding solutions. The problem was referred, for the first time to the second finance commission. But, in spite of the various suggestions of the second finance commission the fundamental problem of increasing states' debt and debt servicing could not be solved. The burden of debt servicing charges continued to increase. Thereafter, a review of the state debt has been the term of reference from the sixth finance commission onwards. It is seen from the above discussion that, while the issue of debt sustainability is a concern across all the states, their heterogeneity in terms of size, level of income, and their financial position measured by various fiscal indicators and ability to raise resources on their own, calls for varied policy initiatives. The severity of debt problem faced by different states need state specific analytical and exhaustive study, as it will have implications on states debt sustainability as well as centre-state financial relations. The present study is an attempt to fill the gap in the study of public debt of the Manipur state specific, under the framework of federal financial problems of India.

Constitutional Framework of Inter-Governmental Borrowing in India

In the literature of public debt we find a fairly developed theoretical framework of public debt in general. The general theory of public debt has given considerable importance to the burden of public debt i.e. the burden of interest on loans and repayments of principal on the economy and people of present as well as future generations. Many of these generalizations have been empirically tested and certain broad guidelines for government public debt policy are recommended. However we do not have economic theory of intergovernmental public debt as yet. Though the theory of fiscal federalism has developed to a high level of sophistication, theory of intergovernmental debt remains neglected. Hence it is necessary to have a closer look into intergovernmental debt operations, based on the general theory of public debt on the one hand and theory of fiscal federalism on the other.

In order to reduce wide inter-state disparities in income, rising revenues etc. intergovernmental borrowing comes the best option available to achieve thee objectives. "Though intergovernmental debt operations can be used to promote these objectives, they are inadequate taken in isolation. However, in the context of the universal presence of vertical federal fiscal imbalance, intergovernmental debt operations become useful supporting tools when used along with other more effective federal fiscal transfers such as tax sharing and grants for achieving these multiple objectives. The first consideration which should be examined in any theory of intergovernmental debt operations is: when should the state governments borrow from the national government and for what purpose. This question invariably assumes that there is a constitutional provision for state borrowing as such, "In the Indian constitution, articles 292 and 293 pertain to borrowing by the government. Under the constitution, the state government can borrow only within the territory of India. The constitution empowers the central government under article 293 to provide loans to the states. Article 293 states as:

Borrowing by states:

1. Subject to the provisions of this article the executive powers of a state extend to borrowing within the territory of India upon the security of consolidated fund of state within such limits, if any, as made from time to time be fixed by legislature of such state by law and to the giving of guarantees within such limits, if any, as may be fixed.
2. The government of India, subject to such conditions as may be laid down by or under any law made by Parliament, make loans to any sector or so long as any limits fixed under Article 292 are not exceeded, give

guarantees in respect to loans raised by any state, and any sums required for the purpose of making such loans shall be changed on the Consolidated Fund of India.

3. A state may not be without the consent of the government of India raise any loan if there is still outstanding any part of the loan which has been made to the state by the government of India or by predecessor government, or in respect of which a guarantee has been given by the government of India or by predecessor government.
4. A consent under clause 3 may be granted, subject to such conditions, if any, as the government of India may think to impose.

Cleary, the Government of India has been providing short term loans in form of ways and means advances and some medium and long term loans from the Consolidated Fund of India to the state governments.

It is generally accepted that there is constitutional provisions to make loans to states. But it was thought that the capital needs of a state would be normally met by its own borrowing. But this assumption has now broken down because of the policy of planned development and so, also the centre-state financial relations are strained. It is sometimes, complained that states have been financially assisted by means that appears to be a doubtful use of Article 293. This Article 293 is a unique provision in our constitution which has no parallel in other federal constitutions. But from the article, it seems that only open borrowing is intended. As the article has been used to advance loans to the states on a large scale, the centre hardly keeps watch over the use of fund. The huge sums are used imprudently. No doubt, the borrowing powers of state have been unduly restricted by the constitution. The constitution does not permit states to borrow from outside India. The constitutional discrimination between the centre and states has been one of the irritants in Federal relations. Given a persistent surge in public debt, it can be nobody's case that the Centre manages its debt better than states' and the latter cannot be borrowing without restrictions. But the states' indebtedness over the seventies and eighties has reached critical proportions leading to successive Finance commissions being entrusted with the task of easing states' debt burden. Even if such constitutional does not exist, extra-constitutional arrangements can be justified for inter-governmental debt operations". In this context there are two major theoretical views in the general theory of public debt which can be adopted for analyzing the inter-governmental debt operations. They are: (1) pay-as-you-go view, and (2) future generations view. The 'pay-as-you-go' view maintains that in normal circumstances capital as well as recurring expenditures should be financed from non plan revenues. However these conditions can be relaxed in three types of situations, namely: (a) when there is an imminent need to incur abnormally high expenditures either once- and- for –all or to cover a limited period of time, (b) when the expenditure involved is likely to yield direct monetary returns to service the loan and to repay the principal, (self-liquidating Loans), and (c) when there is need for incurring huge expenditures to combat depression. Therefore, the proponents of this view maintain that the government should not resort to borrowing for financing public expenditures except in the above mentioned exceptional circumstances. The 'future generations' view maintains that since the benefits from capital expenditure which are proposed to be undertaken by the state governments will be enjoyed mostly by the future generations. It is always appropriate to finance such capital expenditures by borrowing from the national government subject to reasonable terms and conditions of loans. This implies that the capital expenditure programmes will benefit only the future generations because of their long gestation period, and therefore, the beneficiaries, (future generations), should be made to pay for servicing and repayment of such loans. In recent years a third view has emerged under the theory of cost-benefit analysis. This is basically a variant of 'pay-as-you-go' view but has received considerable attention in view of the fashionable treatment the theory of cost-benefit analysis has received in the hand of mathematical economist. There are two variants of the third view: (a) simple cost benefit view, and (b) social cost-benefit view. The simple cost benefit view maintains that when the public works go to benefit only some specific sections of the people, it is only appropriate to finance such public works by borrowing and to acquire the concerned beneficiaries to pay for servicing and repaying debt through special tax measures. The social cost benefit version of the third viewpoint maintains that the orthodox notions concerning self-liquidating expenditures are too confining and are to restrict the intervention of the government in the national economic activity. What is necessary is that capital expenditures which will earn a social return should be financed by borrowing whether they earn a economic or financial return or not. Further it is maintained that it is difficult to evaluate expenditures programmes to be financed by loan in terms of social return, in the long-run it is possible to evaluate the social–cost benefit analysis of certain type of expenditures such as on education, roads and health facilities etc which are of the nature of social and economic infrastructure facilities.

All the above mentioned views cannot be exclusively taken as guideline for inter-governmental borrowings. Because, the relation between the Union government and the state governments in a federation is not commercial or mainly guided by profit/ loss or simple cost benefit considerations. They are partners of a common endeavor to promote social welfare. This however should not be used as an excuse for wasting financial resources obtained through borrowing. Keeping all these considerations in view, we can say that the state governments can borrow from national government for the three exceptional purposes justified by 'pay-as-you-go' view and those justified under the cost-benefit analysis.

The states receive central assistance in three forms: shares in taxes and duties, grants and loans; and there are three institutional processes through which states are receiving funds from the centre, namely (1) on the basis of recommendations of the Finance commission, (2) on the basis of suggestions of Planning Commission, and (3) at the discretion of the Union ministers. It is the plan as well as discretionary transfer by which central loans are given to state governments.

The plan assistance comprises of both conditional grants and non-conditional grants. It is significant to note that grants–loan proportion of the plan assistance was not uniform before 1969 and also the loan component varied from program to program and from state to state.

Even internally the borrowing is subject to limitations as may be imposed by the state legislature under Article 293(1) and if the Union Government has guaranteed an outstanding loan of the state without the consent of the union Government as per Article 293(3). It is argued that restrictions do not obtain in a federation like U.S.A.

It is felt that in a planned economy like India there is need for some restrictions, it should apply only to long–term and medium term borrowing from open market and not to borrowing from financial institutions or to short terms loans for less than one year. In this context, it is quite relevant to quote what the Sarkaria Commission feels "a solution lies in making a distinction between short –term loans under one year and medium and long term loans.

According to the commission, "The union should give it freely to states for borrowing from banks and financial institutions for periods less than one year under clause (4) of Article 293. Since most of these are now nationalized, no irremediable risk could be involved.

What emerges from the ongoing discussion is that, the Indian Constitution sets the basic rules of the country's sub-national borrowing regime. Section 293 forbids state Government from borrowing abroad and requires them, as long as they are in debt to the union government, to obtain central approval for domestic borrowing. The following sources of domestic borrowing are open to the states: Government of India (central plan) loans. These are loans linked with grants in a fixed proportion, as 'block plan assistance' to finance the state plan. Block plan loans and grants under the supervision of the planning Commission consists of two parts: (a) an unconditional part, called 'normal central assistance', whose aggregate size is at the discretion of the central ministry of finance; and (b) a conditional part, called additional central assistance, consisting largely of the onward transmission of donor resources through the centre o the states under various externally aided projects.

After earmarking 30 percent of the normal central assistance for the special category states according to planning Commission formula. (The revised Gadgil formula (1991) gives 60 percent weight to population, 25 percent an inverse measure of per capita income,2.5 percent to tax effort, 2.5 percent to Fiscal management 2.5 percent to national objective and 7.5

percent to special problems.). The block plan assistance to each state, including both normal and additional components, takes place as a standard mix of loan and grant-70/30 for the special category states.

The Constitution of India, article 293, allows state governments to raise loans upon the security of their respective consolidated funds subject to some conditions. Though overseas borrowing by state governments is banned there are no aggregate limits on domestic borrowing. In case the central governments has advanced a loan to a state which is outstanding then that particular state is barred from taking any fresh loans without the consent of the central government. In addition, the central government is empowered by article 360 to declare a financial emergency if financial stability of a state is seen to be threatened. There is no constitutional definition of what constitutes financial stability and this term is open to a variety of interpretations.

By declaring a financial emergency the central government is empowered to take over and completely control the taxation and budgetary revenue processes of a state government. To date this provision of the constitution has never been used and there is a large amount of ambiguity about the course of action if a state government actually defaults on its loans. The fact that many state governments have debt levels that may be unsustainable implies that the central government has not exercised effective control over state government borrowing. Thus it is clearly seen that, while it is the states that determine the demand for debt, it is the centre that controls the supply. As actual borrowing has been historically driven by the supply constraint (i.e. states typically borrow whatever is available), how the central government plays its role as the controller or regulator of state debt has a important bearing on fiscal sustainability at the state level. States have six sources of deficit Financing. These are subject to differing degrees of central control.

The Indian Constitution sets the basic rules of the country's sub-national borrowing regime. Section 293 forbids state Government from borrowing abroad and requires them, as long as they are in debt to the union government, to obtain central approval for domestic borrowing. The following sources of domestic borrowing are open to the states:

(i) Government of India (Central Plan) Loans

These are loans linked with grants in a fixed proportion, as 'block plan assistance' to finance the state plan. Block plan loans and grants under the supervision of the planning Commission consists of two parts: (a) an unconditional part, called 'normal central assistance', whose aggregate size is at the discretion of the central ministry of finance; and (b) a conditional part, called additional central assistance, consisting largely of the onward transmission of donor resources through the centre o the states under various externally aided projects. After earmarking 30 percent of the normal central assistance for the special category states according to planning Commission formula. (The revised Gadgil formula(1991)gives 60 percent weight to population, 25 percent an inverse measure of per capita income,2.5 percent to tax effort,2.5 percent to Fiscal management 2.5 percent to national objective and 7.5 percent to special problems.)

The block Plan assistance to each state, including both normal and additional components, takes place as a standard mix of loan and grant-70/30 for the special category states.

(ii) State Bonds

State bonds are issued to banks and financial institutions through a process managed by the RBI. Bonds from different states are sold at the same time and at the same price. RBI also manages debt servicing for their bonds, and allocates for the purpose funds transferred from the central government, all of which pass through central bank. Thus the Bonds are supported by an implicit escrow arrangement, though not by central guarantee. The amount of borrowing per state is determined by Government of India (GoI) at the start of the year, largely based on precedent, though adhoc adjustment are frequently made in courses of the year to allow for 'additional market borrowing', with room for lobbying.

(iii) Negotiated Loans

These are from public insurance companies and other GOI-Owned financial institutions. The target of such borrowing is set at the time for annual plan finalization.

(iv) Small Savings

Net public Deposits from the central Post office savings schemes with administered interest rates that have been maintained above market rates, along with income tax incentives extended by the centre, are available to be states in which thy accrue partially for general deficit financing purposes and partially to swap with old and more expensive small saving debt under a scheme introduced by GOI loans, but are now accounted for separately.

(v) Provident Funds

Flows into provident and insurance funds are involuntary savings of state government employees at administered interest rates- the net inflow being the difference between deposits of the premium by each account holder, on the one hand and the sum of net loans extended and final payment of maturity (at the time of retirement), on the other.

(vi) Other Public Accounts

In addition to the five sources listed above, states also finance a portion of their accounted fiscal deficits through the public accounts. Besides the provident fund accounts considered in item (v) Public account flows are best understood as accounting transfers, whereby expenditure are booked under a deposit account but actually incurred.

The increase in the balance of public account is then defined as having financed the booked expenditure shows that in fact they may not be incurred in subsequent years as well. The outstanding balance in other public accounts is excluded from debt stock calculations, reflecting that they are largely non-debt creating.

State governments in India raise debt from various other sources also: Ways and Means Advances (WMA): These are short-term (typically for three months) loans provided by the Reserve Bank of India (RBI) to enable states to bridge gaps that could arise for short periods between expenditures and receipts. RBI makes these loans while fulfilling its role as banker to the state governments. The aim is to prevent short-term expenditure and revenue mismatches from causing a disruption in the activities of state governments. Generally speaking these are not considered to be a part of the debt of states as these advances have a life of less than a year. It has been pointed out that many states continuously maintain an overdraft position so such over drafts should in certain cases be considered a part of state debt. From time to time the RBI has been revising the rules and procedures to be followed with respect to these advances. In what follows we continue with the convention of not considering these advances to be a part of states' debt.

Loans from the Central Government

This accounts for the largest proportion of the total loans of states (and their total liabilities). Large part of these loans arise in the process of inter Governmental fiscal transfers through the planning commission. These are loans that are combined with grants that are given to state governments to finance state plans. These loans are largely formula based and thus may have very little to do with a states borrowing capability.

In 1969 it was decided by the National Development Council that each state would receive 30 percent of total central assistance provided on account of the state plans every year, as a grant and the rest 70 percent as a loan. For the special category states (these are all states other than the 14 major states) since the Fifth Plan the pattern of assistance was 90 percent grant and 10 percent loan. Such a system has lead to an accumulation of debt as a consequence of the planning process. Apart from this there are ad hoc loans provided to states under special circumstances. A large part of these loans arise through the process of transfers of resources to state governments from the center and not from a commercial relationship. The principal difficulty arises because plan size (which determines the size of loans from center) has never been linked to sustainable levels of state debt. No state government can or does refuse to take these loans because it does not see itself in a position to repay the loans nor does the central government refuse to give loans to state governments whose financial position is weak.

Gupta has aptly summarized the situation as follows and we quote: "Legally the states are under no obligation to ask for or accept loans from the Union Government. But factually the states are not in a position to exercise their legal freedom to decline Union loans. They can, dare not, forego to undertake the development projects in the states, and are, therefore, willingly compelled to accept the Union loans with or without strings attached to them. And once they accept the loan the process becomes unending. This makes states dependent on the union and, in a sense; it amounts to infraction of state autonomy But such has become the logic of Union-State fiscal relationship that the Union can neither refuse to give loan nor can it bring a distress warrant against the States." These loans have at least to be partly serviced (interest and principal) from the funds received by states in terms of grants in aid or tax shares from the centre (i.e. transfers arising from Finance Commission recommendations). The centre is thus taking back as interest and debt service, funds that are being transferred to the states. Both the creation of the debt is partly formula based and transfer of resources to states is also partly formula based. If these formulae are creating debt for states with no consideration of their repayment ability then the emergence of a fiscal crisis for some states on this count may be unavoidable. This would be especially true in a situation where the dispersion of states' ability to repay loans is increasing due to an increase in the dispersion of growth rates of state domestic products.

There are also other borrowing mechanisms that exist outside the formal framework. First, to circumvent central controls on market borrowing, some states raise fund through special purpose vehicles: the debt off the budget, but debt servicing is through the budget. Such practice became very popular during the course of the 1990s, especially on the part of the better off states. Various order have been issued by GOI and RBI, which would, if implemented, bring off-budget borrowing to an end. Second, states run up arrears. The most striking case of this was in the power sector, where budget constraints were truly soft as states could buy power from central utilities, sell it at loss, and not have to pay for it. Recent changes in the mechanism for paying central power utilities have, to a large extent, closed off this loophole Without analyzing the weakness of the borrowing framework, the study will not be complete and it will be useful for analyzing the problems and prospects of Public debt management in subsequent chapters.

Too much state-level borrowing, especially for the poorer states: This is the most fundamental problem, and is partly a result of the other problem listed below. India's states were already heavily leveraged before the crisis of the late 1990s; since then, then the state-level debt burden has skyrocketed and states now have the highest debt/revenue ratio of any sub-national entities world wide.

The poorer states are particularly indeed, with higher deficit and debt ratios than other states. In the last two year, GoI has wisely controlled the use of small savings for deficit financing by earmarking a significant and increasing portion to retire old high-cost debt to the centre. However, this can only be a temporary solution.

Complex System with Elements of Discretion and Arbitrariness

The borrowing regime is complex with multiple borrowing channels, each with its own rules. There are elements of description and arbitrariness, especially relating to open market borrowings, the allocation of which between states follows no pattern except history.

A New Borrowing Regime for States

In order to avoid the above mentioned problems and, following the Twelfth Finance Commission's (TFC) recommendations that the centre should not act as an intermediary for future lending and allow the state Governments to approach the market directly, a new borrowing regime for the States was put in place. Accordingly, in the Union Budget 2005-06, there was no provision made for Central loans for State Plan Schemes. The Union Budget indicated an amount of Rs.29,003 crore which was to be raised by the States and Union Territories with Legislature directly from the market. Furthermore, as per the TFC's recommendations (also accepted by the Government of India), external assistance would be transferred to the States on the same terms and conditions as attached to such conditions by external funding agencies (making Centre a financial intermediary - without any gain or loss). The States would get the same maturity, moratorium and amortization schedule as the Centre gets from the external lender.

The most important reform of the borrowing regime would be to introduce an aggregate borrowing cap and allow for greater flexibility over the choice of borrowing instruments within the cap. There is thus a strong case, in the short to medium term, the Government of India to impose an aggregate cap on each state, i.e. place an upper bound on the state's annual net borrowing. Within the cap, however, states could be provided with maximum facility for arranging their own borrowing, and be exposed as much as possible to market discipline. Adoption of such an approach would have a disciplining impact on both states and the centre. It would close avenues for bargaining by the states for additional loans, and for the centre to use its discretion to approve additional loans. GoI has in fact already begun to move in this direction. Various steps could be taken to move this reform further forward. The ministry of finance has started to use the borrowing levels specified in the medium-term Fiscal restructuring Plans of the various states as caps on aggregate borrowing.

It has also started to allow greater flexibility with regard to some sources provided it stays within the overall cap. The 2004/05 Union Budget gave states the option to borrow from the market instead of from the central government Nevertheless; there is clearly a long way to go. There is no formula for defining the caps, and no mechanisms for ensuing enforcement. Following are the some of the steps that could be taken to move further in the reform journey on which GoI has already embarked. The first step would be to shift to a formula based approach for defining the aggregate gap for each state. The cap should be based on observables, and not subject to negotiation. It could be defined in terms of debt servicing or debt stock or annual net borrowing as a percentage of GSDP or total revenue receipts in an earlier year. Given the states are now adopting fiscal responsibility acts, the central government could simply adopt and enforce the borrowing targets already legislated by the states. The targets however derived, would need to be below current levels of borrowing for most states, which would force one to define a time period within which borrowing would need to be brought under the cap, and a transitional path.

Once the cap has been decided on, enforcement mechanism are needed, exante and expost. Exante, all resources allocation discussions between the centre and the state would have to be consistent with borrowing being at or below cap.

What emerges from the foregoing discussion is that, Federations around the world show a great deal of variety in their sub-national borrowings regimes. The borrowing by the states of India has grown to unsustainable levels even though it is formally under the control of the centre shows that the actual effective control over sub-national borrowing is far below what the constitution of India allows for. Of the borrowing sources outlined above, only two-loans from GoI (Government of India), itself and market borrowing are clearly under the effective annual control of GoI interest rates independent of credit worthiness. By and large, states all pay the same interest rates for their debt, and have the access to capital market. States typically approach the market together, and it is said that the RBI pushes creditors to buy a mix of state bonds, in particular leaning on them to purchase bonds from states perceived as being less creditworthy; thus the better managed states cross-subsidies the worst managed ones. Such practices enormously weaken the incentives for prudent fiscal behaviour. In 1999, the RBI did allow states to sell bonds on their own specific auctions, up to 35 percent of their total market borrowing allocation; more recently some states have even raised up to 50 percent of their allocation in this way. But this remains only an option, not a requirement, and in fact reliance on state-specific auctions is declining, not increasing. It is also clear that the sub-national borrowing regime needs to be rationalized and simplified. At one extreme, one cold advocate forcing all states to go the market for borrowing, and relying on the markets to discipline the states and punish imprudent policies with worse credit ratings and higher interest rates. However, given the past experience, financially weak state like, Manipur reveals that the weaknesses in their finances invited adverse reaction from the financial markets as manifested in the widening spread on State Government securities and under-subscription to market loans. The under-subscription to the State market loans also brings to the fore various factors that impact State Governments liquidity. Here it is quite relevant to note some of the factors given by World Bank Report factors include: (i) the fiscal health of the State Governments, (ii) the credibility of their prospective policy actions and, (iii) transparency of their budgets. Considering these adverse impacts and the lack of role for a credit markets in the current federal fiscal system, it would be inappropriate and risky to rely solely on this approach such a system. Thus, the consensus in the literatures is for 'market-based' discipline supplemented by rules-based controls.

CHAPTER 2

MAGNITUDE, COMPOSITION AND TRENDS IN THE PUBLIC DEBT OF MANIPUR

The public debt of the economy is considered a very comprehensive measure of the fiscal discipline of the government. However, the absolute magnitude is often misleading because it depends on the size of the economy and the rate of growth over time. Moreover, the amount of public debt and the fiscal deficit are closely related as borrowing represent a pre-dominant source of financing the deficit of the budget. Public Debt is therefore also considered a percentage of the state income to reflect the overall Fiscal health. Unless one understands how debt statistics are defined, and collected, it is not possible to group the new dimensions of the debt problem. Figures on the debt crisis are discrepant not only because of the different system of data collection from which they derive; they also differ according to particular definitions of what is being measured. For assessment and measurement of dimension of public debt, right concepts have to be used and properly measured, use of inappropriate concepts of public debt at the state level can have resulted into misleading target setting and wrong perceptions of the dimension of the debt problem at the state level. Therefore, we need to have a closer look into the magnitude, composition, trends and how State's Public debt is defined in the Indian Federation within the framework of modern theory of fiscal federalism.

Unfortunately, there is no agreement among different bodies on the definition of Public Debt of the state. Before we attempt an analysis of the states' debt position, we would like to address a key issue: what the appropriate measure of debt at the state level is.

The definition used by the state governments differ substantially from RBI which in turn, differs considerably from the concept used in the Discussion paper on subsidies i.e. DPS (1997). The Eleventh Finance commission (2000) uses none of these but has its own definitions. Since the ultimate source of these definitions is the same is the same viz., Finance Accounts of the state government; we can review the exact differences by considering the principal sources of funds given there. They are Public Debt which includes: (a) Internal debt from the state government (b) Loans and advances from central government (c) small savings, provident funds etc; (d) contingency fund (e) reserve funds, bearing interest and not bearing interest (f) deposits bearing interest and not bearing interest and advances (g) Suspense and miscellaneous receipts; and (h) remittances. All these together add up to the total debt and other obligations of the state government. Deducting cash balances and investments from the total debt and other obligations, the net provision of fund is obtained. With a purpose of having unanimity on the definition of composition of state government liabilities, a working group on the methodology and compilation of state liabilities was constituted as per the decision taken in the 14th Conference of State Finance Secretaries (August

2004). Availability of consistent time series data on the liabilities of the Government is of particular importance as it would throw light on their debt servicing capacity. At present, there appears to be no unanimity about the exact level, composition and the methodology for compiling the liabilities of State Governments in India.

Recognizing the various problems associated with the database of the State Government liabilities, the Conference of State Finance Secretaries held at the Reserve Bank, in August 2004, considered and approved the proposal of constituting a Working Group on Compilation of Liabilities of the State Governments. Transparency, reliability and consistency in the fiscal data are crucial for successful management of government finances. The time series data on the liabilities of government is of particular importance as it affects future state of affairs of government finances. At the policy making level as well as at the academic level, a need to streamline the reporting of data on State Government liabilities is increasingly felt. The number of studies making an assessment of the financial health, and the mixed results generated by them, highlight, among other things, the need for having reliable and credible statistics on public debt which are comparable across States, countries and time period. In this regard, the methodology for compiling the data on debt/liabilities of State Governments assumes considerable importance. At present, there appears to be no unanimity about the exact level, composition, and the methodology for compiling the liabilities of State Governments in India. The budget documents of the State Governments do not provide data on their outstanding liabilities. Such data are, however, provided in the 'Finance Accounts' of the State Governments, but these reports are not available in respect of all State Governments on a timely basis.

Present Status

A survey of the existing important publications presenting data on fiscal liabilities shows substantial differences in definition and coverage of liabilities among these sources. This essentially reflects that debt statistics are compiled in an ad hoc manner. This issue needs urgent attention and action. From the above discussion, it is clear that the concepts of public debt and liabilities need clearer definition to avoid confusion and erroneous use. For policy purposes, we can consider them as synonymous. The concept must have grounding in the analytical framework for its effective use in policy making. The most important use of debt or liabilities of a State Government is for assessing its fiscal sustainability. All the available alternative measures of fiscal sustainability require correct measurement of debt and liability of a State Government.

Defining States' Debt

States' debt consists of all liabilities that require payment of interest and or principal by the state government at some future date. In this study, the terms debt and liability have been used interchangeably. Debt is defined to include internal debt, loan and advances from the Centre and all public account liabilities such as provident funds, Reserve funds and deposits. This yields the total of explicit debt. Capital receipts held in suspense accounts, remittances and other miscellaneous receipts which are of a non-debt nature are not included in the debt definition The exclusion of implicit liabilities from conventional debt statistics is based on the presumption that all contingent liabilities are eventually vacated by the solvent borrower with no implication for the financial health of the state government. But a clear idea of the magnitude of contingent liabilities is essential for accurate reflection of the net worth and strength of the public sector. Therefore, two measures of debt are reported: conventional debt normalized by GSDP and augmented measure, which adds on the full extent of contingent liabilities to explicit debt. In this context it is quite relevant to study the recommendations of Working Group on Compilation of State Government Liabilities (RBI). "It is proposed that debt and liabilities be considered synonymous. Accordingly, all borrowings which are repayable and on which interest accrues are recommended to be considered as debt. Alternatively, the practice followed in the Government of India budget may be adopted by the States as well. Thus, total budgetary liabilities are recommended to be decomposed in four categories viz. (i) Public Debt; (ii) Ways and Means Advances (WMA) and Overdrafts (O) from the RBI; (iii) Public Accounts; and (iv)Contingency Fund. The above treatment would be in conformity with the international best practice. As eluded to earlier, the IMF Manual on Government Finance Statistics, 1986, IMF describes government debt 'a stock of liabilities with different time dimensions accumulated by government operations in the past and scheduled to be extinguished by the government operations in future." the above definition of liabilities brings about a closer alignment with that of (Gross Fiscal Deficit) GFD. The remaining discrepancy between computation of GFD and liabilities is essentially on account of certain 'Memo items' (i.e. withdrawal of cash balances, Appropriation to Contingency Fund, Suspense and Miscellaneous and Remittances) which are treated as financing items of the GFD, but excluded from liabilities.

The Group recommends that withdrawal of cash balances may continue to be taken as a financing item of GFD. Cash balances, in any case, do not form part of liabilities. The remaining memo items viz., 'Appropriation to Contingency Fund', 'Suspense and Miscellaneous' and 'Remittances' may, however, be treated as non-debt items and excluded from the computation of GFD and liabilities, with a view to maintaining consistency between the definitions of GFD and liabilities.

The most significant off-budget for state governments is in the power sector. During the 1990s, cash strapped governments were unable to meet their rapidly rising subsidy obligations to the electricity companies. Thus an increasing proportion of power sector losses, which reached almost 1.4 percent of GDP by 1999/00, were met off budget, in large part through arrears to central utilities. If the full amount of the losses or subsidy obligation, were included, the combined state' fiscal deficit increases even more sharply. Therefore, the implicit liabilities that include Off-Budget Borrowings, Contingent Liabilities, Pensions and State Public Sector Liabilities should be excluded from the definition of State Liabilities or Debt. However, it is recommended that they may be disclosed in the financial statement along with estimates of debt. In those cases, however, where it is indicated a priori that the liability for repayment of principal and/or interest payment of the borrowings of special purpose vehicles (SPVs) whose debt servicing would be met by the State Government from the provisions in its budget, the same should be included under the explicit/budgetary liabilities of the State Government As discussed earlier, the coverage of debt should be consistent with GFD. The break-up of GFD is then used to construct a measure of debt in annual flow i.e. Increase in Debt = Increase in [Internal debt (including WMA & OD) (net) + Loans & Advances from the Centre (net) + Small Savings & PF etc. + Deposits (net) + Reserve Funds (net) + Contingency Fund (net).

It is also felt that the demarcation of Public Debt into Internal Debt and Loans & Advances from the Centre can be done away with. It is instead proposed to report a single major head viz. Public Debt and include all items currently reported under Internal Debt and Loans & Advances from the Centre as minor heads within it. The final definition of Liabilities, as proposed by this working group comprises of the following items as proposed by the Working Group:

1. Public Debt (including WMA & OD from RBI)
2. Small savings, PF etc
3. Reserve Funds
4. Deposits
5. Contingency Fund

However, in another definition given by Shroff and Dholkia is that the debt of a state government should be measured as the total debt and other obligations i.e., the total of items of (a) to (h) of the Working Group's proposal less the cash balances at any point of time.

Considering the consistency requirement and in a democratic federal set up, the most relevant concern is the use of right concepts and their proper measurement which can make a difference as discussed above.

Institutional Arrangements

Working group proposed that all the data relating to the liabilities of State Governments may be published in the budget documents of the respective State Governments. The State Governments should also bring out quarterly, if not monthly reports on their accounts and liabilities. It may be noted that data to be provided in the Statements 1 to 7 relate to three years viz., the budget estimates of the current year, revised estimates of the previous year and 'accounts' data of the year before. It may also be noted that these 'accounts' data provided in the budget documents are un-audited figures and that ideally, audited data should be used which would ensure comprehensive accuracy of the relevant magnitudes. As indicated above, timely availability of audited data on State Government budgetary transactions, however, continues to be beset with some difficulties, which need to be addressed by the concerned entities at the earliest. The CAG may also compile and publish the audited data on liabilities in addition to the Finance Accounts of the States. The Group, however, suggests that the non-availability of audited data should not delay the reporting of data on liabilities as per the 'accounts' (un-audited), revised estimates and budget estimates of the latest years.

In order to facilitate the process of data compilation, the Group recommends the following: Reserve Bank of India (RBI) will provide the data on outstanding market borrowings to the State Governments. The Central Government may provide the details regarding the loans from Centre to the State Governments as also Special Securities issued by the States to NSSF. The data on borrowings from banks and financial institutions and any other such transactions may be provided by the State Governments. Till such time that the State Governments are not in a position to publish the requisite data on their outstanding liabilities in their budget documents, all the above data may be furnished by the concerned institutions to the RBI, as a transitional measure, to enable consolidation and publication. As alluded to earlier, the RBI's annual Study on State Government provides, inter-alia, State-wise detailed data on the budget estimates of the current fiscal year, the revised estimates of the previous year and the 'accounts' (un-audited) data of the year before.

This is the only publication to provide such updated data in respect of all the State Governments on a regular and timely basis.

Keeping this in view, the Group recommends that the RBI should compile the (latest available) 'accounts' (un-audited) and (revised and budget) estimates of liabilities of all the State Governments and publish the same in its regular annual publication on State Budgets, from the viewpoint of data dissemination and to facilitate academic and policy research. The CAG may provide the latest available audited data on liabilities and the same could also be reported by the RBI in its annual study on State budgets, along with the 'accounts' (un-audited) and the revised estimates and budget estimates of more recent years.

Trends in the Outstanding Debt of State Governments

The outstanding debt of states stood at Rs 26783 cores in as in end of march1980-81, increased to Rs 1163834 cores during 2005-06. Table 2.1 presents data on the composition and trend in outstanding debt of the states. The large and growing fiscal deficit of the states particularly since 1990s, led to the accumulation outstanding debt of the states. The main reason for the rise in the indebtedness of the states has been the increasing of loans taken by the states. As a result of increasing indebtedness, the states are spending more for debt servicing.

Table 2.1
Outstanding Debts of States Governments

(Rs. in crore)

Year (As at end of march)	*Internal Debt*	*Central Loans*	*Provident Funds*	*Total*
1980-81	4443	16980	5360	26783
1981-82	6182	19080	6393	31655
1982-83	5607	23557	7811	36978
1983-84	6540	26979	9680	43199
1984-85	8323	30555	11857	50735
1985-86	-8049	38786	14520	61355
1986-87	9065	43702	17108	69875
1987-88	10854	49534	20792	81180
1988-89	-13213	56222	24337	93772
1989-90	16194	64139	29516	109849
1990-91	-19274	73521	35359	128155
1991-92	23270	82979	40780	147030
1992-93	26853	91626	49886	168365
1993-94	30933	101239	55819	187992
1994-95	35875	115865	65359	217100
1995-96	43895	130618	96376	250889
1996-97	51338	148373	88372	288103
1997-98	-59289	171737	102871	333897
1998-99	77190	202795	123378	403364
1999-00	126346	235514	154018	515877
2000-01	181623	243910	176539	602073
2001-02	249069	254884	196571	700524
2002-03	333753	253952	221216	798921
2003-04	429063	268069	226368	923500
2004-05	535380	256265	250660	1042305
2005-06	628181	261201	274451	1163834

Source: Data are derived from RBI: State Finances, A study of Budgets: various issues and Handbook of Statistics of State Finances (RBI)

Table 2.2
Composition of Outstanding Liabilities of state Governments

Item (As at end – March)	*1981*	*1991*	*2000*	*2005*	*2006*
1. Internal Debt of which: (i) Market Borrowings (ii) Special Securities issued to NSSF (iii) Loans from Banks and FIs	16.5	15.0		57.8	59.8
2. Loans and Advances from the Centre	63.3	57.4	45.2	15.6	13.4
3. Public Accounts (i to iii) (i) Small Savings, State PF, etc. (ii) Reserve Funds (iii) Deposits & Advances	19.8	26.8	29.9	26.6	26.6
Contingency Fund	0.14	0.8	0.3	0.1	0.1
Total Liabilities (1 to 4)	100	100	100	100	100
Total Liabilities	26783	1,28,155	5,09,529	10,29,174	11,67,866

Source: Same as Table 2.1 [calculated from Table 2.1]

Table 2.2 presents the composition of outstanding debt of states at the end of March 1981, 1991, 2000, 2005 and 2006. The composition of the outstanding debt has undergone significant changes over the last two and half decades. The share of loans from the centre shows a sharp decline with corresponding increase in the share of special securities issued to NSSF, market borrowing and loans from the banks and other financial institutions. More importantly, the composition of the outstanding debt has undergone significant structural changes between March 2000 and 2005. The principal reason for this has been the phenomenal growth in Loans from National Small Savings Fund (NSSF). This was on account of the high growth in net small savings collections during the period and also on account of the policy changes in the sharing of the net collection between centre and states. Earlier these collections were shared-net between the centre and states in the ratio of 20:80. From 2002-03 onwards the entire net collections have been made to the states As a result, by 2005 loans from NSSF have become the single most important component of outstanding loans of the states, accounting for about 31percent of the total. Significantly, reserve funds and deposits and advances have constituted 19.8 percent in 1981, and declined to 13.2 percent in 1991 and in the subsequent years it continued to constitute around 15 percent. Loans from NSSF would remain the dominant component during 2006, followed by market borrowings and loans from the Centre. Other important sources of debt are small savings, State provident funds, and loans from banks and financial institutions (6.8 per cent) government Finances, RBI.

Table 2.3
Debt/GDP ratio and Annual Growth of Debt of State Governments

Year (As at end-March)	*Amount (Rs. Crore)*	*Annual Growth (percent)*	*Debt/GDP*
1991	1,28,155	-	22.5
1992	1,47,030	14.7	22.5
1993	1,68,365	14.5	22.5
1994	1,87,875	11.6	21.9
1995	2,16,473	15.2	21.4
1996	2,49,535	15.3	21.0
1997	2,85,898	14.6	20.9
1998	3,30,816	20.8	21.7
1999	3,99,575	27.5	23.0
2000	5,09,529	16.6	26.1
2001	5,94,148	16.6	28.3
2002	6,90,747	16.3	30.3
2003	7,86,427	13.9	32.0
2004	9,13,376	16.1	33.0
2005	10,29,174	12.7	32.9
2006	11,67,866	13.5	32.7

Source: RBI: A study of budgets, 2007-08

Table 2.3 highlights the debt/GDP ratio of the state governments. The Debt/GDP ratio of the state governments at end-March 1991 was placed at 22.5 per cent of GDP. The debt-GDP ratio, which was at a low of 20.9 per cents at end-March 1997, rose sharply to 32.7 per cent as at end-March 2006 but declined to 30.8 per centos at end-March 2007 (Table 2.2). The outstanding liabilities of State

Governments are budgeted at Rs.13, 78,663 crore as at end-March 2008 with the debt-GDP ratio placed at 29.8 per cent. With the concern for the sustainability of the high level of debt, State Governments in their (Fiscal Responsibility Legislations) FRLs[1] have placed limits on the level of debt to be achieved within a stipulated time frame. The TFC has also recommended for 30.8 per cent debt-GDP ratio to be achieved by the States at the end-March 2010 from the viewpoint of ensuring debt sustainability in the medium-term. Furthermore, the TFC has recommended overall cap on borrowings (3 per cent of GSDP) to be achieved by the State Governments by the end of 2009-10.

The outstanding public debt of Manipur has increased from 29.82 crores in 1972 to 3193.19 crores in 2005. It has increased by more than 107 times. This is evidently clear from Table 2.4. It is also clear that the outstanding central loans to the state have increased to from 28.54 crores in 1972 to 1480.50 crores in 2005. It has increased by more than 51 times. It is also clear from the table that Public debt of Manipur increased from 2982 crores in 1972 to 79.48 crores in 1981. Since then it increased to 236.30 crores in 1988, it has further increased to 3193.19 crores in 2005. Thus within 17 years, Manipur's public Debt has increased by more than 13 times. Thus, this rapid increase in the Public Debt of the state government shows its ever increasing dependence on loan finance particularly on the central Government.

1 The FRLs Act, 2003 (as amended), which became effective from July 5, 2004 mandates the Central Government to eliminate revenue deficit by March, 2009 and to reduce fiscal deficit to an amount equivalent to 3 per cent of GDP by March, 2008

Table 2.4
Outstanding Debt of Government of Manipur

(Rs. in crore)

As on 31st March	*Internal debt*	*Central Loans*	*Provident funds. etc.*	*Total*
1972	-	28.54	1.29	29.82
1973	1.11	34.25	1.47	36.83
1974	3.11	43.60	1.68	48.39
1975	6.10	51.40	1.95	59.46
1976	6.50	58.08	2.46	67.05
1977	10.95	49.17	2.87	62.99
1978	12.26	49.96	3.27	65.50
1979	13.12	55.59	3.87	72.59
1980	20.35	57.19	4.68	82.21
1981	28.44	45.21	5.84	79.48
1982	76.87	44.72	6.83	128.41
1983	29.37	115.79	9.21	154.36
1984	43.51	124.31	11.66	179.48
1985	51.91	123.51	15.73	191.15
1986	52.65	140.78	20.61	214.04
1987	56.52	140.49	25.08	222.09
1988	66.41	141.02	28.93	236.36
1989	81.59	146.34	53.37	281.30
1990	104.63	157.34	60.83	322.80
1991	136.08	191.55	73.74	401.37
1992	169.91	184.39	93.27	447.56
1993	170.26	177.10	114.75	462.11
1994	182.77	176.90	133.04	492.71
1995	206.10	182.56	137.77	526.43

As on 31st March	Internal debt	Central Loans	Provident funds. etc.	Total
1996	245.20	196.01	128.66	569.87
1997	317.9	227.70	153.13	698.72
1998	505.23	286.34	172.22	963.79
1999	734.23	334.90	179.65	1248.78
2000	653.98	398.83	467.67	1520.48
2001	819.69	548.64	559.10	1927.43
2002	963.66	460.35	600.4	2065.76
2003	605.38	907.44	552.94	2140.07
2004	765.98	835.49	538.60	2814.94
2005	774.58	1480.50	559.85	3193.19

Source: Finance Accounts, Government of Manipur (1972-73 to 2005-06)

Table 2.5
Outstanding Debt of Manipur Government
(in percentage form)

As on 31st March	Internal debt	Central Loans	Provident funds, etc.	Total
1972	–	95.71	4.33	–
1973	3.01	92.99	3.99	100.00
1974	6.43	90.10	3.47	100.00
1975	10.26	86.44	3.28	99.98
1976	9.69	86.62	3.67	99.99
1977	17.38	78.06	4.56	100.00
1978	18.72	76.27	4.99	99.98
1979	18.07	76.58	5.33	99.99
1980	24.75	69.57	5.69	100.01

As on 31st March	*Internal debt*	*Central Loans*	*Provident funds, etc.*	*Total*
1981	35.78	56.88	7.35	100.01
1982	59.86	34.83	5.32	100.01
1983	19.03	75.01	5.97	100.01
1984	24.24	69.26	6.50	100.00
1985	27.16	64.61	8.23	100.00
1986	24.60	65.77	9.63	100.00
1987	25.45	63.26	11.29	100.00
1988	28.10	59.66	12.24	100.00
1989	29.00	52.02	18.97	100.00
1990	32.41	48.74	18.84	100.00
1991	33.90	47.72	18.37	100.00
1992	37.96	41.20	20.84	100.00
1993	36.84	38.32	24.83	100.00
1994	37.09	35.90	27.00	100.00
1995	39.15	34.68	26.17	100.00
1996	43.03	34.40	22.58	100.00
1997	45.50	32.59	21.92	100.00
1998	52.42	29.71	17.87	100.00
1999	58.80	26.82	14.39	100.00
2000	43.01	26.23	30.76	100.00
2001	42.53	28.46	29.01	100.00
2002	46.65	22.28	29.06	98.00
2003	28.29	42.40	25.84	96.53
2004	27.21	29.68	19.13	76.03
2005	24.26	46.36	17.53	88.15

Source: based on above Table 2.4

In Table 2.5, the further decomposition of outstanding debt of Manipur into Internal debt, central Loans and provident Funds etc. is listed. Traditionally, the major part of the state's debt was owed to the centre. Over the years, the share of central loans which was 95.17% in 1972, declined to 34.83% in 1982 decreased to all time low as low as 22.28% in 2002 and increased to 46.36% in 2005. Over the years, the share of Central loans in the states' debt has declined. This has been due to: i) increasing recourse to market loans and loans from financial institutions, ii) changes in the accounting procedure in 1999-00 under which proceeds from small savings which were treated as loans from Centre are being shown as part of internal debt iii) debt swap scheme initiated in 2002-03 under which states have been permitted to repay their high cost loans to the centre through additional market borrowings and a portion of small savings receipts (Special securities issued to National Small Saving Funds (NSSF) have emerged as the most important source of funds for the states, accounting for more than 50 percent of incremental liabilities in 2002-03.

It is clear from the data presented in Table 2.6 that the gross loans of Manipur increased from Rs 8.70 Crores in 1972-73 to 367.59 Crores in 2005-06. The debt servicing charges (Repayment and interest payment) of the state increased from Rs 3.16 Crores in 1972-73 to Rs 535.85 Crores in 2005-06. The percentage of net to gross loans changed from 63.79 in 1972-73 to 38.29 in 2005-06. The table also reveals that in many cases the ratio of net to gross Central loans is very low and in certain cases such flow has been negative This indicates heavy debt burden on the states which can be called a situation of debt trap.

Table 2.6
Amount of gross and net Loans taken by the Government of Manipur

(Rupees are in crores)

Years	*Gross Loan*	*Repayment*	*Interest*	*Net Loans*
1972-73	8.7	1.7	1.46	5.55
1973-74	23.87	12.3	1.87	9.69
1974-75	13	1.94	2.14	8.92
1975-76	10.67	3.08	3.01	4.58
1976-77	56.84	60.89	3.61	-765
1977-78	30.06	27.55	3.46	-95.62
1978-79	17.39	10.3	3.93	3.15
1979-80	37.39	22.69	1.69	12.93
1980-81	116.91	119.65	4.99	-7.72
1981-82	150.48	101.55	6.02	42.91
1982-83	70.81	44.86	5.74	20.21
1983-84	59.55	34.42	7.78	17.33
1984-85	99.13	87.48	11.54	0.12
1985-86	70.56	47.67	11.35	11.54
1986-87	39.68	31.63	15.68	-7.63
1987-88	36.78	22.52	18.1	-3.84
1988-89	75.27	30.34	17.48	27.45
1989-90	116.45	74.96	22.86	18.64
1990-91	217.12	138.55	32.06	46.51
1991-92	290.05	243.86	31.09	15.09
1992-93	385.61	371.07	44.53	-29.99
1993-94	203.5	172.9	48.9	-18.29
1994-95	196.69	162.97	51.77	-18.06
1995-96	158.33	114.89	92.18	-48.74
1996-97	789.22	524.15	966.15	701.08

Years	*Gross Loan*	*Repayment*	*Interest*	*Net Loans*
1997-98	853.15	568.16	181.31	103.68
1998-99	90.52	93.8	131.96	-181.31
1999-00	44.24	57.05	177.16	-178.03
2000-01	43.25	35.34	191.41	-183.5
2001-02	118.19	158.8	158.8	-173.13
2002-03	1460.15	1385.85	215.33	-141.03
2003-04	538.6	841.83	266.43	408.44
2004-05	367.59	298.32	237.53	140.74

Source: Finance Accounts, Government of Manipur (1972-73 to 2004-05)

Direction of Central Loan

The centre provides loans to states for both plan and non-plan purposes. They are intended for development and non-development purposes. While Plan-Loans for Plan Schemes comprise loans for:

- Central Plan Schemes
- Centrally Sponsored Schemes
- NEC Schemes etc.

Non-Plan Loans are mainly for purchases of fertilizers and other agricultural inputs; house building allowances; modernization of police force; education-National Loan Scholarship Schemes. They are for tiding over temporary difficulties, which comprise of the following:

- State Plan Schemes
- Share of small savings collections
- Loans to cover gap in resources

- Ways and Means Advances
- Others etc.

From the foregoing chapters, it is clear that the magnitude of central loans to the states has increased enormously during the study period under which the states have been assisted by the central government largely in the form of loans for plan purposes. Loans are advanced to the states for development activities which mean economic activities intended to create productive capacity in the economy which yield income. The activities are again classified into plan and non-plan. Plan loans are sanctioned on the recommendations of the planning Commission. They fall outside the Revenue Budget. The non-plan loans are provided on the recommendation of the Union Ministries, particulary the Ministry of Finance. They are discretionary in nature but they are included in the Revenue Budget. The plan and non-plan loans may be for development and non-development activities do not correspond to plan and non-plan activities, rather they are inter-mingled.

The plan and non-plan purpose classification serves only the financial and administrative convenience. They are not useful for economic evaluations. The Sixth Finance Commission classified central loans into development and non-development loans. The development purpose include according to it, loans for irrigation, development of agriculture and allied activities, community development and National Extension schemes, industrial housing and such other purposes., on-development purpose include loans for Rehabilitations scheme and loan for Relief Works. They also include adhoc loans for clearing unauthorized overdrafts, ways and means advances and loans meant for filling up the gap in revenue expenditure of the states.

Sometimes, the purpose justifies the loan financing. The theory provides economic reasoning for raising loans by the government for financing certain types of expenditure instead of taking resort to taxation and grants. There are two approaches towards the theory of public debt.

The modern approach considers public debt as important fiscal instruments for regulating the functioning of the economy. It forms the basis of credit in the modern society. It should be utilized for stabilization and economic growth of the country. The loans can be raised for economic growth of the country. The loans can be raised for economic growth and for social welfare.

It is clear that tax-versus loan financing is decided on the nature of the public expenditure and the latter should decide whether the State government should be assisted by the Central Government with loan for financing the normal expenditure of the state governments. Such expenditure consists of non development expenditure. Central loans should be advanced for productive activities. This will specify the purpose for which loans should be taken by the State government from the Central Government.

Table 2.7
Compositions of Central Loans to the Government of Manipur

(Plan and Non-Plan)

Year	*Plan Loan*	*Non-Plan Loan*	*Total*
1972-73	6.05	1.02	7.07
1973-74	5.26	8.5	13.76
1974-75	8.04	0.09	8.13
1975-76	6.95	0.17	7.12
1976-77	0.98	0.15	1.13

Year	*Plan Loan*	*Non-Plan Loan*	*Total*
1977-78	2.56	0.07	2.63
1978-79	2.99	4.59	7.58
1979-80	2.82	11.08	13.9
1980-81	3.81	38.25	42.06
1981-82	3.95	18.03	21.98
1982-83	7.75	69.34	77.09
1983-84	8.82	3.56	12.38
1984-85	8.96	1.2	10.16
1985-86	10.2	32.73	42.93
1986-87	10.15	6.72	16.87
1987-88	11.42	1.71	13.13
1988-89	15.63	2.89	18.52
1989-90	7.6	19.86	27.46
1990-91	9.48	47.61	57.09
1991-92	12.11	3.94	16.05
1992-93	13.13	44.97	58.1
1993-94	18.81	53.77	72.58
1994-95	17.54	5.35	22.89
1995-96	20.83	-	20.83
1996-97	28.79	13.81	42.6
1997-98	54.77	78.53	133.3
1998-99	168.79	102	270.79
1999-00	70.04	18.08	88.12
2000-01	39.86	1.05	40.91
2001-02	67.55	3.64	71.19
2002-03	451.85	573.09	1024.94
2003-04	85.28	-	85.28
2004-05	5.06	940	945.06

Source: Finance Account Government of Manipur (1972-73 to 2005-06)

Table 2.7 reveals that Manipur received Rs 7.07 cores as central loans in 1972-73 which have risen to reach the maximum of 1024.94 in 2002-03 and fell down to 85.28 crores in 2003-04, again it has risen to 945.06 crores in 2004-05. Table 2.8 highlights Composition of Plan and Non-Plan Loan in Total Loan. Out of the central loans received in 1972-73, Plan loan and Non-plan loans amounted to Rs. 6.05 cores and 1.02 respectively. Plan loans constituted 85.57 of the total loans advanced in 1972-73. The percentage of plan loans to total central loans has fallen to 39.45 percent 1977-78 up to 1981-82. The percentage of plan loans to total central Loans was only 97.43 percent in 2000-01, but it fell down to 0.54 in 2004-05, which was the lowest percentage so far. The recent decrease in the plan loan is not difficult to find. Manipur being a Special Category state has been getting plan funds mainly in the form of grants. This has resulted to less transfer of loans from the centre to Manipur for Plan Purposes. This is the reason why non-plan loans of Manipur have been much larger than the plan scheme.

Table 2.8
Composition of Plan and Non-Plan Loan in Total Loan

Year	*Plan loan to total loan as %*	*Non-plan to total loan as %*	*Total*
1972-73	85.57	14.43	100
1973-74	38.23	61.77	100
1974-75	98.89	1.11	100
1975-76	97.61	2.39	100
1976-77	86.73	13.27	100
1977-78	97.34	2.66	100
1978-79	39.45	60.55	100
1979-80	20.29	79.71	100

Year	*Plan loan to total loan as %*	*Non-plan to total loan as %*	*Total*
1980-81	9.06	90.94	100
1981-82	17.97	82.03	100
1982-83	10.05	89.95	100
1983-84	71.24	28.76	100
1984-85	88.19	11.81	100
1985-86	23.76	76.24	100
1986-87	60.17	39.83	100
1987-88	86.98	13.02	100
1988-89	84.4	15.6	100
1989-90	27.68	72.32	100
1990-91	16.61	83.39	100
1991-92	75.45	24.55	100
1992-93	22.6	77.4	100
1993-94	25.92	74.08	100
1994-95	76.63	23.37	100
1995-96	100	0	100
1996-97	67.58	32.42	100
1997-98	41.09	58.91	100
1998-99	62.33	37.67	100
1999-00	79.48	20.52	100
2000-01	97.43	2.57	100
2001-02	94.89	5.11	100
2002-03	44.09	55.91	100
2003-04	100	0	100
2004-05	0.54	99.46	100

Source: based on Table 2.6

There is no denying the fact that the classification of central loans into plan loans and non plan loans does not correspond to the categorization of the central loan to development and non development loan purpose loans and at the same time some plan loans, e.g. loans for social security and welfare, loans for police-modernizations of police force etc. are non-development loans. Many a time, even non-development purpose loans create a basic infrastructure which are absolutely necessary for economic development. The beneficial consequences of expenditures on construction of schools, hospitals, roads, bridges, flood control etc add to the efficiency of production and thus they are less productive than those expenditures which yield revenue directly. Thus all expenditures incurred out of public debt are productive of public welfare.

In thc words of Dr. Bhargava, R.N., "sometimes expenditure that does not produce revenue might be more essential and productive of greater welfare, for example, expenditure incurred to check epidemics or famine relief or to fight a war to defend the freedom of the country. Public debt incurred for financing expenditure of this type is really more productive of welfare, it is not correct to call public debt incurred for these purposes as unproductive," on the other hand the plan loans which are advanced for water supply, drainage and flood control schemes are not self liquidating schemes. The irrigation projects are also not self-liquidating because the government is not getting return from those who are benefited by these projects. So is the case with loans advanced to agriculturist which is held up due to various factors more particularly to due to political reasons of losing votes at the poll. Despite these, the development and non-development purposes loans or plan or non-plan loans are advanced to the state/states for its/their economic growth-oriented policies and for the policies to further the social welfare of the people.

Table 2.9
Plans Loans taken by the Government of Manipur

(Rupees in crores)

Year	*State Plan Schemes*	*Central Plan Schemes*	*Centrally Sponsored schemes*	*NEC schemes*	*Total*
1972-73	1.9	NA	NA	-	6.05
1973-74	2.04	NA	NA	-	5.26
1974-75	5.15	0.34	1.84	-	8.04
1975-76	6.32	0.08	0.45	-	6.95
1976-77	1	0.12	0.5	0.13	0.98
1977-78	1.85	0.01	0.64	0.08	2.56
1978-79	2.15	0.05	0.14	0.06	2.99
1979-80	2.54	0.09	1.08	0.12	2.82
1980-81	2.67	0.04	0.29	0.05	3.81
1981-82	3.45	0.1	2.13	0.18	3.95
1982-83	5.43	0.63	0.77	0.14	7.75
1983-84	7.74	0.09	1.8	0.21	8.82
1984-85	6.91	0.04	1.13	0.2	8.96
1985-86	8.69	0.04	0.69	0.26	10.2
1986-87	8.67	0.63	1.09	0.14	10.15
1987-88	9.5	0.04	0.62	0.78	11.42
1988-89	14.6	0.01	11.6	0.39	15.63
1989-90	5.6	0.02	0.69	0.81	7.6
1990-91	8.13	0.07	1.09	0.62	9.48
1991-92	10.74	0.03	0.62	1.06	12.11
1992-93	11.26	0.01	1.06	0.23	13.13
1993-94	16.44	-0.96	0.23	1.54	18.81
1994-95	16.31	-	1.54	0.63	17.54
1995-96	18.82	0.03	1.95	0.03	20.83
1996-97	23.69	4.3	0.64	0.16	28.79
1997-98	53.36	0.04	0.61	0.75	54.77
1998-99	167.73	-	0.79	0.27	168.79
1999-00	68.16	0.24	1.61	0.01	70.04
2000-01	37.91	-	1.26	0.68	39.86
2001-02	65.67	-	1.78	0.1	67.55

Year	*State Plan Schemes*	*Central Plan Schemes*	*Centrally Sponsored schemes*	*NEC schemes*	*Total*
2002-03	450.49	-	0.9	0.45	451.85
2003-04	83.76	-	-	1.52	85.28
2004-05	0.29	-	3.76	1	5.06

Source: Finance Accounts, Government of Manipur (1971-72 to 2005-06)

Government never spends its revenue which is unproductive from the social welfare point of view. This is the approach of the modern theory of public debt also. What is disturbing is not the amount of the loan but its proper utilization which is not satisfactory.

Table 2.10
Non-Plan loans taken by the Government of Manipur

(Rupees are in crores)

Year	*Share of small savings collection*	*Loans to cover gap in resources*	*Ways and Means Advances*	*Others*	*Total*
1972-73	-	-	-	-	1.02
1973-74	-	-	-	-	8.5
1974-75	0.02	-	-		0.09
1975-76	0.12	-	-		0.17
1976-77	0.11	-	-		0.15
1977-78	0.03	-	-		0.07
1978-79	0.09	4.45	-	0.06	4.59
1979-80	0.07	-	11	0.01	11.08
1980-81	2.9	13.06	22.24	0.04	38.25
1981-82	0.09	-			18.03
1982-83	0.09	66.29	0.16	2.79	69.34

Year	Share of small savings collection	Loans to cover gap in resources	Ways and Means Advances	Others	Total
1983-84	0.16	2.56	-	0.84	3.56
1984-85	0.4	-			1.2
1985-86	0.62	15	15.5	1.61	32.73
1986-87	0.96	-	4.99	0.79	6.72
1987-88	0.96	-	-	0.75	1.71
1988-89	1.99	-	-	-	2.89
1989-90	16.81	-	-	-	19.86
1990-91	6.63	32	8	0.98	47.61
1991-92	2.4	8	-	-	3.94
1992-93	2.66	-	41	1.31	44.97
1993-94	3.65	-	49	1.11	53.77
1994-95	4.94	-	-	0.41	5.35
1995-96	12.99	144	-		
1996-97	0.18	1.13	-	2.51	13.81
1997-98	12.6	-	63	2.93	78.53
1998-99	13.79	-	0.08	3.22	102
1999-00	17.99	-	-	0.09	18.08
2000-01	-			1.05	1.05
2001-02	-	-	-	3.64	3.64
2002-03	-	-	572.68	0.41	573.09
2003-04	-	-	-	-	-
2004-05	-	-	331	609	940

Source: Same as Table 2.7

Table 2.10 presents a picture of Non-Plan Loans taken by the Manipur government. The amount non-plan loan taken by the Manipur was 1.02 crores in 1972-73, increased to 8.50 in next year, then it had fluctuated within a short range of 0.7 to 4.59 in the following five years, it has risen to 11.08 in 1979-80, since then it has fluctuated within wide range. In 2000-01, it reached the maximum of 940.00 crores. It is also clear from the table, that the share of small savings which was 0.02 in 1974-75 reached to 17.99. The state also takes loan to cover the gap in resources which was 13.06 cores in 1980-81 and144.00 cores in 1995-96. Ways and Means advances are also taken as a part of non-plan loans. The fluctuations in the amount non-plan loans taken by state have been mainly due to the fluctuations in the amount of these two loans (loans to cover the gap in resources and ways and means advances). It is seen from the table that both loans to cover the gap in resources and were not taken in the year 1997-98 to 2005-06. Both loans to cover the gap in resources and ways and means advances were not taken in the year 2000-01 so the non-plan loan amounted to only 1.05 cores in 2000-01. The sudden increase in non plan in 2003-04 and 2004-05 was mainly due to the increase on the ways and means advances only taken by the government.

Table 2.11
Debt/NSDP data of Government of Manipur

Year	*NSDP*	*Outstanding Debt*	*Debt/NSDP*
1972-73	63.61	29.82	58.4
1973-74	82.23	36.83	63.75
1974-75	95.56	48.39	51.79
1975-76	101.82	59.46	51.81
1976-77	105.17	67.05	45.42
1977-78	121.63	62.99	41.2
1978-79	126.42	65.5	32.84
1979-80	159.82	72.59	50.09

1980-81	199.56	82.21	50.78
1981-82	242.02	79.48	52.1
1982-83	256.35	128.41	51.35
1983-84	303.98	154.36	50.24
1984-85	344.49	179.48	40.99
1985-86	372.25	191.15	39.01
1986-87	426.04	214.04	44.36
1987-88	541.77	222.09	44.65
1988-89	605.83	236.36	46.26
1989-90	634.08	281.3	46.76
1990-91	723.01	322.8	39.94
1991-92	867.69	401.37	37.73
1992-93	957.11	447.56	37.28
1993-94	1156.97	462.11	37.72
1994-95	1305.97	492.71	37.14
1995-96	1412.23	526.43	45.35
1996-97	1510.65	569.87	42.27
1997-98	1881.51	698.72	51.47
1998-99	2125.21	963.79	68.5
1999-00	2954.11	1248.78	68.54
2000-01	2954.11	1520.48	68.12
2001-02	2813.64	1927.43	68.5
2002-03	3014.08	2065.76	68.54
2003-04	3141.73	2140.07	68.12
2004-05	3564.35	2814.94	78.97
2005-06	5454.06	3193.19	58.55

Source: NSDP- Statistical Abstract (various issues) Government of Manipur

Table 2.11 reveals that the outstanding debts of Manipur constituted 58.40 percent of the states' net domestic product at the end of 1972-73 and 58.55 percent at the end of 2005-06. The outstanding debt as percentage of NSDP were highest in the year 2004-05 The above ratio demonstrates that the concern expressed in various circles regarding the burden and magnitude of the debts loses much of its substance. The table highlights also that the outstanding debt in terms of its percentage to states' net domestic product has fluctuated, the debt/NSDP ratio which was lowest as 37.14 percent in 1994-95 raised to 78.97 percent in 2004-05, which was the highest Debt/NSDP ratio. The increase had been spectacular from 1998-99. It shows that state finance is certainly in bad shape. The principle of sound finance requires that the rate of growth of central loans should be less than the rate of growth of NSDP.

CHAPTER 3

AN OVERVIEW ON DEBT CRISIS; AN EVALUATION OF CAUSES

While the financial crisis of the union government has so far been averted, there is little sign that the burden of debt servicing faced by many states has become less burdensome, indeed for many debtor states the situation has been deteriorating. The situation is likely to deteriorate further in view of the implementation of Sixth Pay Commission. In this chapter, the debt crisis and the problems and the prospects of public debt management will be studied in the light of the above statement.

What Led to Sharp Deterioration of State Finances?

There is a vast fiscal literature, which has investigated the various factors leading to the deterioration of state finances. The inability to contain wasteful expenditure including subsidies, reluctance to raise additional resources and competitive reduction in taxes are attributed as the main causes of fiscal deterioration. Another study identifies the increase in the share of non developmental expenditure, particularly rising interest payment, and slanginess of central transfers as the principal causes of deterioration of state finances.

Increasing debt service payments and inadequate returns from government spending are major factor behind the deteriorating fiscal conditions of states. Since there is no link between the capacity to borrow and returns on services provided by the government, there does not exist much incentive for the government to levy appropriate user charges. In fact, the lack of connection between fiscal health and ability to borrow has encouraged fiscally irresponsible behavior on the part of the states. Detailed analysis of fiscal trends by Govind Rao (2002) and Shanker Acharya (2002), illustrate the implementation of the fifth pay commission awards as a major cause of sharp deterioration in state finances.

Genesis of the Fiscal Crisis

A slow secular deterioration in fiscal performance over the 1980s and 1990s was catalyzed into a state-level fiscal crisis by the Fifth Central Pay Commission pay awards in the 1990s. We use the term 'fiscal crisis' not to be alarmist, or to suggest faltering macroeconomic performance but to convey the sharp deterioration in state-level fiscal performance witnessed in the late 1990s-deficits rose, the state level debt stock, which had been declining, started rising rapidly, and off-budget liabilities also grew quickly. There was also a liquidity crunch, not in the economy, but in the state governments, who started finding it more difficult to pay bills, and even salaries. State governments themselves certainly perceived that they were facing a crisis. Like many other states Manipur government department of finance wrote White papers in June, 2002 to apprise legislator and the public of the extent and causes of the serious financial crisis of the early 1990s, not in the nature of the crisis, but its impact: just as the Bop crisis of 1991 gave rise to a decade of central government reforms push, so the state level fiscal level fiscal crisis gave an enormous impetus to reforms at the state level.

The Fifth Central Pay Commission awards, phased in by the states starting in 1997/98, resulted in real wage increases of about 30 percent. Pensions, which had been growing slightly faster than the rate of GDP through the 1990s, started to grow much more rapidly in the late 1990s as the Commission ruling indexed pensions to real wages.

There are four reasons why we call a fiscal crisis:

- First, the sharp deterioration in budgetary fiscal indicators, even sharper if off-budget liabilities are included.
- Second, the liquidity shock as state governments struggled to pay the salary increases they had agreed to State governments, with limited borrowing sources, experienced severe liquidity problems in the late 1990s. The RBI of India runs an emergency overdraft facility for state governments. There were many reports in the late 1990s of state government closing the treasuries since they no_longer had the cash to pay the bills. State government distress is also evident from their borrowing from the employee through the impounding salaries increase to provident funds. Borrowing from the provident funds tripled in nominal terms between 1997/98 and 1999/00 (Reaching 0.9 percent of GDP). State governments lacked the cash to pass on the promised salary increases to workers, and

were only able to do so by promising to pay part of the increase with interest when the employee retired.

- The sense of crisis: The influential magazine India Today February issue titled its cover: *States going broke: Bankruptcy Stalking a Collapse of Public services*. And it was not just a case of by the media state government used this languages.
- The impact of the crisis: Just as the BOP crisis 1991 gave rise to decade of central government reforms push, so the state level fiscal crisis gave an enormous impetus to reforms at the state level.

Was there Really a Fiscal Crisis at the State of Manipur?

To understand, was there really a fiscal crisis at the state of Manipur, and the factors responsible for the increasing fiscal imbalance in the state it is necessary to analyze, transfer of resources from the centre to the state of Manipur, and the trends of revenues and fiscal expenditures over the years.

Table 3.1
Fiscal Health of the State Manipur

(Rs. in crore)

Year	*Revenue deficit*	*Primary Deficit*	*Gross Fiscal Deficit*
1991-92	54.34	(-)43.85	(-)75.92
1992-93	73.85	(-)36.50	(-)67.58
1993-94	101.39	45.59	1.05
1994-95	129.89	58.33	9.43
1995-96	83.74	(-)10.32	(-)62.10
1996-97	72.90	(-)47.21	(-)104.76
1997-98	112.62	(-)91.34	(-)156.93

Year	*Revenue deficit*	*Primary Deficit*	*Gross Fiscal Deficit*
1998-99	70.57	(-)110.86	(-)189.76
1999-00	106.02	(-)17.00	(-)108.28
2000-01	(-)278.07	(-)511.91	(-)643.01
2001-02	(-)78.22	(-)48.75	(-)226.01
2002-03	(-)161.00	(-)149.00	(-)340.00
2003-04	(-)87.00	(-)6.00	(-)249.00
2004-05	(-) 44.00	(-)71.00	(-)286.00

Source: CAG Report and government of Manipur, White paper and C & AG Report, 2005 (from 2000-01 Onwards) Deficit (-), Surplus (+)

The Table 3.1 highlights the fiscal health of the state over a period of fifteen years. The Table 3.1 reveals that there had been revenue surplus during 1999-2000 but the state started experiencing a series of revenue deficit in the following years. The revenue deficit rose to Rs 278.07 core in 1999-2000 but it fell down in subsequent years. It is clear from the table that state had been suffering from a series of primary and gross fiscal deficit over a period of fifteen years with the exception of surplus in 1999-2000 by registering Rs.511.91 crore and Rs.643.01 crore respectively.

It would be useful to analyze the trends of federal fiscal transfer. We now that federal transfer in India mainly consists of share in Central Taxes; loans centre from and Grants from the centre. The following Table 3.2 highlights the composition and trends in Transfer of Resources from the Centre to the State of Manipur.

Table 3.2
Transfer of Resources from the Centre to the State of Manipur

(Rs in crore)

Year	*Share In Central Taxes*	*Loans From the Centre*	*Grants from the Centre*	*Gross Devolution and Transfer*	*Net Devolution and Transfer*
1981-82	7.5	42.1	70.5	120.1	63.1
1982-83	8.5	22.0	80.3	110.8	86.6
1983-84	9.3	15.6	96.4	121.3	113.5
1984-85	9.8	9.8	111.5	131.1	124
1985-86	12.5	10.2	147.4	170.1	151.5
1986-87	55.9	42.9	152.5	251.3	219.5
1987-88	69.0	16.9	154.4	240.3	213.5
1988-89	82.5	13.1	173.7	269.3	243.5
1989-90	102.0	18.4	203.9	324.3	301.3
1990-91	81.8	29.2	216.6	327.6	300
1991-92	112.0	58.8	242.9	413.7	388.6
1992-93	132.6	16.1	282.1	430.8	306
1993-94	158.3	51.5	284.5	494.3	418.7
1994-95	161.5	72.5	370.5	604.5	513.6
1995-96	181.4	22.9	336.8	541.1	506.5
1996-97	165.8	23.6	452.5	641.9	613.4
1997-98	231.8	33.3	502.9	768	714.2
1998-99	310.8	132.8	475.9	919.5	804.8
1999-00	331.7	146.5	502.8	981	849.7
2000-01	387.8	74.9	599.4	1,062.10	994
2001-02	163.5	236.9	790.4	1,190.80	1,055.50
2002-03	141.2	504.2	954.9	1,600.30	961.5
2003-04	224.4	857.7	1,197.00	2,279.20	1,796.80
2004-05	224.4	481.8	1,111.60	1,817.00	1,333.40

Source: RBI, "The Handbook of Statistics on the Indian Economy", (2005)

It is clear from Table 3.2 that state's share in central taxes and Loans had fluctuated in short ranges and had remained almost constant during 1980-81 to 1996-97, but it increased in the subsequent years. On the other hand, grants from the centre have been continuously rising since 1990-91. The Gross and Net Devolution and Transfer from the Centre to the State had remained almost constant in the first our years but it started increasing gradually in the subsequent years except a minimum decline in 1994-95. From the foregoing discussion, it is clear that the state of Manipur faced financial crisis in the 1990s.

White paper of Finance department, Government of Manipur rightly quoted that, "The state finances which was already under strain in the beginning of the 1990s deteriorated inexorably from 1999-2000. The present fiscal stress is the outcome of the cumulative impact of past policy decisions and initiatives". In fact, sharp deterioration over the past decade can be largely attributed to:

- Growth of revenue expenditure outstripping revenue receipts with the miss-match sharply increasing in more recent years, particularly after the revision of pay scales on the pattern of Fifth Pay Commission's Recommendations with payment of salaries w.e.f 1.1.1996. Similar revision was made for pension also.
- Losses incurred on capital expenditure on projects and investments in public sector undertakings that have proved to be unviable and unproductive causing continuous drain on scarce resources for their maintenance and operations.
- Lack of buoyancy of states tax revenue.
- Inability of State's Government to significantly increase the States non-tax revenue.

- Digression of resources in connection with ethnic clashes, grant of ex-gratia and rehabilitation of displaced persons.
- Increasing obligation of public debt and increasing quantum of borrowing to meet State's revenue expenditure requirements.
- Meeting of Debt obligations on borrowings made by corporate bodies/banks etc.
- Serious cash flow crisis due to the critical fiscal imbalance compelling the State Government to resort to ways and means advances and overdrafts from the Reserve Bank of India almost continuously.

To understand why state is under fiscal stress and problems arising from the growth of public debt of the state government, it would be quite relevant to study the problems and prospects of public debt management as determined by the architecture of Indian fiscal federalism.

Debt Management

Public debt of a states affects the economy in numerous ways., in itself, it is neither good or bad; the nature and extent of the impact depends upon many factors; such as the purpose for which loans have been advanced, their terms and condition, their structures and the maturity structure and maturity mix, their types and interest rates, the debt management policy and the general economic and social condition. Broadly speaking, the impact of loans depends on how the debt is managed. The way in which the debt is managed and the success achieved will directly affect source of security, banking legislations the conservation programmes and many other matte of public policy that country has been accustomed to determine with little reference to their effects upon the federal finance.

The increasing public debt has created the problem of public debt management. Besides, it affects states entire financial system, the process of development and relative welfare of the state, thus the problem of debt management has become an inalienable part of the overall task of co-coordinating the various limbs of state finance in order that the state could pursue certain pre-conceived goals of fiscal action with a measure of certainty and success. An attempt is made in this chapter to study the problems and prospects of debt management especially in the light of the requirement of Manipur Economy.

What is Public Debt Management and Why is it Important?

Public debt management is the process of establishing and executing a strategy for managing the Government's debt to raise the required amount of funding, pursue its cost.

In the words of C C. Abott, "By management of debt is meant the choice of debt forms and proportionate amounts of the different types used, the selection of the pattern of debt maturities, the amount of debt placed with different classes of holders, the decision to repay or refund maturing obligations, the refunding terms offered, the treatment given to classes of debt and different types of bond holders, determination of the provisions attached to new bond issues, adaptation of new issues to the needs of the perspective holders, policies pursued in the retirement or creation of new debt and relative weights given to all these maters in the government's fiscal policy".

In a broader macroeconomic context for public policy, governments should seek to ensure that both the level and the rate of growth in their public debt are fundamentally sustainable over time and can be serviced under wide range of circumstances while meeting cost/risk objectives. Government debt management share fiscal and monetary policy advisors' concerns that public sector indebtedness remains on a sustainable path and that a credible strategy is in place to reduce excessive levels of debt.

The management of Government finances has been in a state of continuous development over the last four decades. This development can be traced largely to the changing tasks o the state and thus of the government. The changes were not merely in the stylc but also in the substance of economic management. Debt management should ensure that the fiscal authorities are aware of the impact of government financing requirements and debt levels on borrowing costs.

The Problem of Debt Management

The problem of debt management arises mainly because the existing debt continuously matures and government must find some techniques of refinancing it. The problem of debt management may exist even when the government does not create any new debt as prof. J.M. Buchanan, has emphasized "debt management takes place even when no debt is created and no old debt is being retired in net terms".

There are two schools of thought of debt management policies; one school is of the opinion that debt should be managed in such a way that minimizes its effect on the economy. As Harris observes "the problem of debt management is largely that of keeping the debt burden at minimum, the concern is with the rate of interest paid, the maturity schedule, the tailoring issues to market needs and the rate of repayment".

By comparison the other school, which is known as the broader concept of debt management, believes by using facets of debt management to utmost in effecting the economy in the manner desired. Representing the later school, Warren. L. Smith points out the nature of public debt management as 'all measures' that affect the size and composition of stock of outstanding claims against the Federal Government.

Role and Objectives of Debt Management

Every Government faces policy choices concerning debt management objectives, its preferred risk tolerance, which part of the government balance sheet those managing debt should be responsible for, how to manage contingent liabilities, and how to establish sound governance for public debt management. The economic performance of any government depends in a significant degree upon the management of its finances, how it taps its sources of revenue and how it utilizes these. To generate adequate finances and to put these to proper use in accordance with a certain well-thought-out strategy for socio-economic development of the economy is indeed a major responsibility of the government. Sound financial management is the key to success in this context.

On many of these issues, there is increasing convergence in the global debt management community on what are considered prudent sovereign debt management practices that can reduce vulnerability to contagion and financial shocks. These include (a) recognition of the benefits of clear objectives for debt management; (b) a limit on debt expansion; (c) the need to carefully manage refinancing and market risks and the interest cost burdens; (d) the necessity of developing a sound institutional structure and policies for reducing operational risk, including clear delegation of responsibilities and associated accountabilities among government agencies involved in debt management; and the need to carefully identify and manage the risks associated with contingent liabilities.

Public debt management problems often originate in the lack of attention paid by policy makers to the benefits of having a prudent debt management strategy and the cost of weak macroeconomic management and excessive debt levels. In the first case, authorities should pay greater attention to the benefits of having a prudent debt management strategy and the costs of weak macroeconomic management and excessive debt levels. Therefore, in the first case, authorities should pay greater attention to the benefits of having a prudent debt management strategy, framework, and policies that are coordinated with a sound macro policy framework.

Two important objectives of debt management requires in the context of planned development of states are (1) to promote savings and provide more funds for investment in the public sector without impinging on the private sector, and (2) to ensure large borrowing and debt requirement without frustrating the objective of maintaining development with stability in the economy.

The first objective of debt management requires a debt policy capable of tapping the funds from all possible sources in the economy. A variety of debt instruments should be deployed to suit the requirements of different types of investors. The debt policy should be so flexible as to offer the terms such as the interest rates and maturities suitable to the conditions prevailing in the money market and capital market. In this process of drawing funds to the public sector, it is necessary to see the private is not adversely affected.

The second and perhaps the most important objectives of debt management is to support the economic objective of development with stability. The loan operations should support and not disturb the objective of development with stability.

Thus, the problem of debt management is not merely those of creating the debt for financing the deficit in the budget and managing the securities market but its objectives are achievement of a faster rate of economic\ growth, the maintenance of structure of interest rates in the organized sector of the money and capital markets, minimization of the cost of servicing the debt. It should be clear from the foregoing discussion is that the main common objectives of debt management is to keep the debt burden at minimum level, which is possible only with the help of suitable structure of interest rates, by the minimization of the of servicing the debt and attracting sufficient funds into the states to maintain faster economic growth with stability.

Against the background of the objectives of debt management in a developing economy stated above, we shall examine the techniques of debt management in financially weak states like Manipur. However, in economically backward states debt management has obvious limitations. Whereas it has come to be recognized as an independent instrument of economic policy in advanced economies; in undeveloped economies it is not such overwhelming importance. But in an economy where money and capital markets are fully developed and the banking sector plays a predominant role in the government borrowing programme, debt management has the claim to be regarded as an important instrument of economic policy.

After having been established, the theoretical base of public debt management to evaluate the impact of public debt in general, now it is pertinent to examine its relevance in the context debt management of state's debt under intergovernmental relations and its impact of public debt management (Management of central loans) on the state. The theories can be adopted in this field with certain modifications taking into view the nature of the debtor and creditor, here both being governments, central government and state government. Both Governments serve the same purpose because the development of the country as a whole is the collective responsibility of the Central and the state Governments. In this context, it is quite relevant to mention what D.M Nanjundappa emphasized, 'The states debt to the centre is essentially like international debt. There is nothing wrong in depending on central loans, but the point is the criteria applicable to the management of India's external debt ought to apply to the management of states, debt to the centre. On the other hand, Government of India's internal debt stands on a different footing. Failure to understand this distinction conceptually leads to misunderstanding which has serious consequences for policy making".

Once we draw a sharp line of demarcation between Central debt, on the other hand, and the state debt on other. It would be logical to maintain debt retirement is no problem in the case of central debt which involves mere transfer of purchasing power from the tax payer to the owner of government of India securities who receive interest. While the secondary burden of interest transfer is admitted, this may be conceded to be of minor character. Most European countries have been following the logic of this argument. They regard their public debt as perpetual. Perpetual debt with no maturity has great advantages for a developing economy. It can avoid the burden of heavier taxes which otherwise be necessary to retire the debt. A loan without maturity provides a safe form of investment for low-income and medium income groups and also a safe and regular income to institutional investors.

Domar, in defending perpetual debt, argues that tax rates necessary to service a given debt must diminish with rising national income. So, according to him, the debt need not be retired; the solution to the debt problem should lie in trying to find ways of achieving a growing national Income. But, with a perpetual debt, there is the problem of heavy incidence of interest payment as a constant, if not rising charge on revenues.

The above arguments suggest a policy of rapid repayment of loans in order to reduce the annual leakage of interest payments from domestic revenues in future. A future tax obligation is the obvious implication of loan but future taxes as well as future benefits are likely to be heavily discounted. If a state rises a loan to finance a long tem project, it should have the corresponding means to pay the service charges. Amortization should provide for the replacement of an asset, so that any new loan should be used for the creation of new assets in addition to the that is replaced. But the position in most of the states (Out of 25) is just the contrary as the repayment and the interest obligations on the outstanding debt of the centre to the centre exceeded the new loans sanctioned.

If the new loan is used to repay the old debt, it becomes perpetual or non-terminable debt resulting in unsound debt management. This is exactly what has happened in most of our states. From this we may question whether it is desirable for every state government to have a debt limit. The logic of debt limitation is to prevent the piling up of burdensome debt service charges which eat into revenues and hamper flexible financing. Each states government, therefore, has to determine the percentage of total revenue which can be diverted to debt service without impairing the proper discharge of its normal functions.

Debt Sustainability

The growing government deficits and rising state's debt obligations in both advanced states and underdeveloped states during the eighties drew considerable attention to the issue of sustainability of public debt. In simple terms,' debt sustainability is defined as the ability to maintain a constant debt-GDP ratio over a period of time. Sustainability is challenged when the debt-to-GDP ratio reaches an excessive value.

In addition to debt-GDP ratio there are various other which light on whether the fiscal policy is sustainable or not. A study of budgets, 2007-08 by RBI, noted that, "an important issue relating to sustainability of debt is the concern about the ability of the State Governments to service their debt obligations." Over the years, large revenue deficits have led to large fiscal deficits and spiraling debt resulting in the emergence of a vicious cycle of deficit, debt and debt service payments for most of the State Governments. The consolidated level of debt of the State Governments relative to GDP has increased significantly from 22.5 per cent at end-March 1991 to 32.7 per cent at end-March 2006. Such increase was more prominent during the period 2001-05. In the context of sustainable level of debt, the Eleventh Finance Commission recommended that the proportion of interest payments (IP) to revenue receipts (RR) should be reduced to 18 per cent as compared to the then average of 22 per cent.

The TFC report, however, mentioned that from 2000-03, the average ratio in respect of seventeen States, out of which Manipur is also one state was above 18 per cent, of which eleven States were above 22 per cent. Thus, in terms of interest payments-revenue receipts criterion, TFC concluded that seventeen out of twenty-eight states had unsustainable debt. A Study on debt sustainability undertaken by the Reserve Bank of India had emphasized the measures for expenditure compression, improvement in own revenue collection effort and several institutional changes to contain the problem of state level debt in India. Important measures of institutional changes included enactment of FRL for making the process of fiscal discipline legally binding, introduction of guarantee ceilings, participation in the Consolidated Sinking Fund and the Guarantee Redemption Fund. It is noteworthy that the FRLs[1] of several State Governments include provisions for caps on the debt- GSDP ratio as well as State guarantees. For ensuring sustainability of debt in terms of a stable debt to GSDP ratio, generation of a primary surplus is a necessary condition, given that the rate of growth of nominal GSDP and nominal rate of interest on the debt stock are equal. In a situation of primary deficit, the debt stabilization condition requires that rate of growth of nominal GSDP is greater than the nominal rate of interest on the debt stock. In this context, it is important to note that despite an improvement in major deficit indicators of the State Governments, the primary balance of many of the States, and consequently at the consolidated level, continues to be in deficit.

1 The FRLs, 2003 (as amended), which became effective from July 5, 2004 mandates the Central Government to eliminate revenue deficit by March, 2009 and to reduce fiscal deficit to an amount equivalent to 3 per cent of GDP by March, 2008

Table 3.3
Distribution of states on the basis of debt as percentage of GSDP (in 19998-99 and 2002-03)

Percentage	*1998-99*	*2002-03*
>60	Sikkim (64.2)	Orissa (62.9), HP (63.3), Mizoram (81.6), Sikkim (60.3)
50-60	Mizoram (58.40), Nagaland (50.9), HP (55.9)	Bihar (55.3), Arunachal Pradesh (55.5), JK (53.8), Nagaland (52)
40-50	Arunachal Pradesh (40.2), JK (48.0), Manipur (44.7)	Punjab (48.5), Rajasthan (45.4), West Bengal (41.2), Manipur (43.1)
30-40	Bihar (33.1), Goa (34.2), Orrissa (37.8), Punjab (34.6), Tripura (37.2)	Gujarat (33.9), Kerala (36.3), MP (32.3), UP (39.1), Assam (33.9)
20-30	Andhra Pradesh (20.3), Assam (23.2), Haryana (21.1), Kerala (27.1), Meghalya (23.4), Rajathan (8.9), West Bengal (26.2)	Meghaya (32.2), Tripura (37.8), Uttranchal (32.4), Andhra Pradesh (28.9), Chastisgarh (25.5), Goa (28.2), Haryana (27.9), Jhakhand (24.3), Karnataka(25), Maharastra (21), Tamil Nadu (24.6)
10-20	Gujara t (18.1), Karnataka (17.5), MP (18.6), Maharastra (13.1), Tamil Nadu (16.4)	

Note: *Figures in bracket are the actual percentages.*

Source: Figures for 1998-99 from EFC and Figures for 2002-03 from TFC.

Table 3.3 indicates that there has been massive increase in the Debt-GDP ratios across the states during the short period of four years between 1998-99 and2002-03. The overall debt GDP ratio for all states increased from 19.6 percent to27.8 percent. While Sikkim was the only state for which debt GDP ratio exceeded 20 percent in 1998-99, there is not even a single debt state with less than 20 percent GDP ratio by 2002-03. The growth in burden in states like Orissa (from 37.8 to 62.9), Bihar (from 28.9 to 45.4), Rajasthan (from 28.9 pent to 45.4 percent), U.P (from 28.o to 33.9), Gujarat (from 18.1 to 33.1) and Tamil Nadu (from 23.2 to 33.9) among the major states and among the special category states Mizoram (58.4 to 81.6) and Arunachal Pradesh (40.2 to 55.3), have been phenomenal and in the case of Manipur (from 44.7 to 43.1), there has been decrease in debt-GDP ratio, which is a sign of increase in fiscal sustainability during the period. An important point emerging from Table 3.3 is that in 1998-99 most of the states with high Debt-GDP ratios were relatively small states whose debt burden, though a serious matter per se, did not affect the overall debt burden of the states and consolidated debt of the states in a significant manner. By 2002-03, the situation has significantly changed in the sense that several major states have debt levels in relation to their GSDP, that are very high and which may have serious implications for their fiscal sustainability and also for their overall fiscal sustainability.

Debt is essentially the aggregate of borrowings made by the government to its fiscal deficit over the years. Therefore, higher the fiscal deficit larger would be additions to the debt stocks. It is quite apparent that from the empirical evidence that interest payments have been the key factor causing sharp increases in state's gross fiscal deficit and rapid growth in outstanding debt of state governments. Thus, efforts to contain growth in debt accumulation or to bring state government on a sustainable path would require a drastic reduction in the interest burden.

The debt position of state governments depends not only on the absolute level of their outstanding liabilities but also various indicators which determine the sustainability of the debt. This section assesses the sustainability of the debt of State Governments in terms of burden of interest payments and maturity pattern of State Government securities and issues arising in the context of liquidity management by the State Governments Ways and Means Advances Debt limits: The burden of debt service charges which sets the debt limit depends upon two factors: (1) average interest rate paid and (2) the average period of maturity of loans. This is the theoretical debt limit which can possibly be altered, owing to the exigencies of rapid economic development, by either lowering the average rate of interest or by extending the period of maturity, or both.

There is bewildering variety as regards the period of maturity. There is need for nationalizing the debt management and evolve an order out of wide variety of interstates and periods of maturity. While fixing the rate, the Government of India should not deal with the states are partners in the big enterprise of national development and there is no justification for charging the states more than the cost of borrowing. A study of budgets undertaken by RBI noted that, "the TFC had emphasized the need to determine borrowing limits for each State taking account of borrowings from all sources including small savings and States' public accounts and reserve funds". Several countries have debt and deficit rules at the sub-national level. In the US, all but two States have laws requiring balanced budgets and limits on rising of debt by the States. Nine provinces and territories of Canada have fiscal rules with balanced budgets requiring them to take debt only for the purpose of financing investment projects. Debt ceiling can serve as a useful adjunct to deficit rules. In practice, debt ceilings have been driven by the concern about reducing high debt levels and are generally chosen on the basis of experience of the individual countries.

Ravindra Dholkia also noted that, it is necessary to examine whether the debt is also within "tolerable" or "manageable" limit. Since market acceptance is not the criterion to follow in this case. This is because the centre borrows on behalf of states and passes on the borrowing to states in India. States are not required to tap the market directly. Thus effectively the centre stands guarantee for all states. Debt is said to be tolerable if servicing does not impose disproportionately heavy burden on the revenues of a state. A state can tolerate interest burden up to what proportion of its total revenues? After informal discussion with senior government officials, politicians, business executives and researchers, we have come to the conclusion that a state can tolerate up to one fifth of its revenues going regularly for meeting its interest obligation.

Interest Payments Burden of State Governments

The stock of outstanding debt for the centre and the states showed a sharp increase over the years. The debt to GDP ratio of centre increases over the years. The debt to GDP ratio of centre increased from 40.44 to 63 percent between 1981-82 and 2002-03. During the same period, the increase in the debt ratio of the state was from 16.77 to 27.80 percent. However, the percentage point increase in the state debt to GDP ratio was lower than that of the centre. It is to be noted that growth of interest payments of the states, which was lower than that of that of the centre during the decade of 1980s, surpassed it during the 1990s (Table 3.4). The divergence has further widened between 2000-01 and 2003-04. During this period, when the centers' interest.

Table 3.4
Debt profile and effective Rates of interest

(percent)

Year	*Debt to GDP Ratio*		*Effective Rates of interest and Spread*		
	Centre	*States*	*Centre*	*States*	*Spread*
1981-82	40.44	16.77	5.35	6.01	0.66
1985-86	49.46	19.30	6.62	6.62	0.00
1990-91	55.31	19.39	8.02	8.02	1.18
1994-95	53.18	18.22	9.22	9.22	2.91
1995-96	51.03	17.86	9.29	9.29	2.59
1996 97	49.38	17.80	9.81	9.81	2.24
1997-98	51.12	18.47	9.71	9.71	2.65
1998-99	52.22	19.64	10.01	10.01	2.75
1999-00	52.72	21.69	10.12	10.12	3.09
2000-01	55.53	23.67	9.73	9.73	2.58
2001-02	59.87	25.71	9.20	9.20	3.35
2002-03	63.14	27.80	9.02	9.02	2.94
2003-04 RE	62.59	29.30	7.99	7.99	4.24

Source: RBI Annual Reports and RBI Study on State Finances (various issues)

Table 3.5
Growth of interest payment: Centre and States

	Centre	*States*	*Difference*
1981-82 to 1989-90	23.79	21.90	-1.89
1990-91 to 1994-95	19.96	22.01	2.06
1995-96 to 1999-2000	15.46	18.48	3.01
2000-01	10.04	14.46	4.41
2001-02	8.20	20.90	12.69
2002-03	14.67	12.22	-2.45
2003-04 RE	1.08	19.71	18.63
2000-01 to 2003-04	8.50	16.82	8.32

Source: Same as Table3.4

The divergence has further widened between 2000-01 and 2003-04. During this period, when the centre's interest payment grew at the rate of 8.50 percent per annum, the rate of growth of states, interest payment remained to be as high as 16.82 percent despite a lower growth of fiscal deficit and outstanding debt of states compared to centre during the same period. Between 2000-01 and 2003-04, the growth of all states' fiscal deficit was 6.55 percent when it was high as high as 10.23 percent for the centre. The stock of outstanding debt growth was also much lower at 5.42 percent for the state for the centre during the same period. It is the accumulated debt of the past contracted at a very high rate by the state governments compared to the centre which has failed to bring down the interest cost of debt in a significant manner for the states. As the average cost of the state debt of the state government remains much higher than that of the central government and percentage point reduction in the average cost of debt for the states was much less significant compared to that of the central government, one needs to explore the reason for this.

The interest rate category-wise distribution of outstanding market loans of both centre and states reveal that the structure of outstanding market loans of the state government is heavily skewed towards high cost loans compared to that of central government (see Table 3.6). For the year 2002-03, loans bearing interest rate of and above 13 percent constituted 19.65 percent of the outstanding loans of states as against 5 percent in the case of the central Government. In the case of interest range of 12.00-12.99, the states' share of Loans is higher at 23.5 percent as against 18.56 percent in the case of the centre. From the distribution of debt structure according to interest category for the year 2002-03, one can infer that if the debt swap scheme has to make an effective dent on the average cost of borrowing it needs to be restructured by taking into account the interest rate category of debt below 13 percent as well as for the purpose of swapping, particularly the share of loans falling under the 12.99 percent inter-state category.

The debt of interest category of 12 percent and above constituted 43.15 of the outstanding debt of the state government in the year 2002-03. One has to take note that in 2003-04, the debt structure of states has undergone an alteration wherein the share of the high interest rate category (13 percent and above) of outstanding market Loans declined to 12.26 percent. However, the combined share of market loans of above 12 percent interest rate in the total outstanding market loans of states remains as high as 29.25 percent in the year 2003-04.

In a segmented credit market, the weighted average coupon rates o state government securities are much higher than that of central government. This is one of the reasons for the states' high average cost of debt vis-à-vis the centre. Also, in the market until recently, no auctioned based market principles were adopted to conduct state's governments market borrowing operation. Reform in the states, market borrowing programmed was introduced in 1997. As a part of this reform, states were allowed to enter into the market via the auction and tap method to enter into the market via the auction and tap method to auction between 5 and 35 percent of the allocated market borrowing at the discretion of the state.

Table 3.6 Interest Rate category-wise Distribution of outstanding market Loans for the Year 2002-03, 2003-04 and 2006-07

Although, the borrowing operation in a limited scale is going on under the auction based market principles for the states since then, the effect on the average cost of debt will only be visible in the medium term, depending on the volume traded via auction and tap system and the maturity period of auction-based debt. Some of the states have preferred not to adopt the flexible auction method and to avoid the risk of under subscription; the tap tranche method was introduced during 2001-02. Under this method, borrowing for all states together are raised, indicating a total targeted amount without notifying the amounts of individual states.

It is encouraging to note that in the year 2003-04, all the states entered the market and traded in government securities through the auction principles could mobilize resources at a lower rate than the tap tranche method. Thus, development of the debt market, innovations in the method of borrowing and maintaining the optimal maturity structure of state debt will be the key concerns of state debt management in medium term. However, due to higher economic growth and the favorable interest rate environment in the recent years, the debt to GSDP ratio of the States has declined in the recent period. It is also important to recognize the large

Table 3.6
Interest Rate category-wise Distribution of outstanding market Loans for the Year 2002-03, 2003-04 and 2006-07

Interest rate Range (in percent)	Centre (Rs. Crore)	Percent Distribution	States (Rs. Crore)	Percent Distribution	Centre (Rs. Crore)	Percent Distribution	State (Rs. Crore)	Percent Distribution	State (Rs. Crore)	Percent Distribution	State (Rs. Crore)	Percent Distribution
	2002-03				2003-04				2006-2007			
5.00-5.99									33.825	14.8	33,825	13.9
6.00-6.99									58,563	25.6	58,564	24.1
Less than 7	57062	8.47	19585	14.72	223153	27.07	70915	39.51	-	-	-	-
7.00-7.99	79654	11.82	11030	8.29	110541	13.41	11029	6.15	49,601	21.7	59,638	24.6
8.00-8.99	29643	4.40	8004	6.02	29638	3.60	8004	4.46	8,004	3.5	18,791	7.7
9.00-9.99	51992	7.72	5411	4.07	51744	6.23	5412	3.02	5,412	2.4	5,412	2.2
10.00-10.99	84572	12.55	14563	10.94	83537	10.13	14560	8.11	14,563	6.4	14,468	6.0
11.00-11.99	212243	31.49	17062	12.82	186344	22.61	17062	9.51	17,062	7.5	16,934	7.0
12.00-12.99	125047	18.56	31269	23.50	107135	13.00	30485	16.99	26,148	11.4	25,959	10.7
13.00 and above	33692	5.00	26142	19.65	32222	3.91	21994	12.26	15.722	6.9	9,186	3.8
Total	673905	100	133066	100	824314	100	179464	100	2,28,98	100	2,42,7777	100

Source: RBI,Annual Reports(2002-03,03-04,05-06)

hump in repayments which will take place during 2012-13 to 2015-16 due to high amount of borrowings during 2002-03 to 2004-05 under the Debt Swap Scheme (DSS). This will require a larger quantum of gross borrowings and can put an upward pressure on the interest rates at which the State Governments borrow, which may further destabilize the debt sustainability condition. It may be mentioned that the State Governments have budgeted interest payments as ratio of revenue receipts for 2007-08 at 16.9 per cent against the TFC target of 15 per cent for the year 2009-10. The State Governments may make efforts through fiscal restructuring to contain their debt at sustainable level.

Table 3.7
Internal loans taken by the Government of Manipur

(Rs. in Lakh)

Year	*Market Loans*	*Ways and Means Advances*	*LIC Loans*	*Others*	*Total*
1972-73	110.88	-	-	-	110.88
1973-74	137.5	812.69	-	2.57	952.76
1974-75	353.93	60	5	-	418.93
1975-76	-	239.13	14	-	253.13
1976-77	304.27	5151.64	15	11.62	5482.53
1977-78	168.57	2459.49	-	1.92	2629.98
1978-79	193.2	650.71	22	-	843.91
1979-80	220	1794.88	41.59	136.78	2173.66
1980-81	252.4	6874.55	19.6	100.35	7268.89
1981-82	305	12260	67	28.49	12613.09
1982-83	330	-1450.76	58	26.49	-1027.27
1983-84	390	3758.9	52	24.37	4231.27

Year	*Market Loans*	*Ways and Means Advances*	*LIC Loans*	*Others*	*Total*
1984-85	909.2	7002.92	42	205.96	8170.08
1985-86	798	846	48	138.68	1824.68
1986-87	742.5	-	55	417.58	1208.08
1987-88	797.51	-	92	362.04	1214.55
1988-89	977	502	41	718.37	2289.37
1989-90	1143	5164.87	74	229.92	6578.79
1990-91	1103	9322.05	-	2502.3	13001.35
1991-92	1213	22943.93	43	78.75	24235.68
1992-93	1452.4	26585.61	69	937.82	29018.83
1993-94	1505.02	6604.4	75.4	1255.59	9434.01
1994-95	1400	10796.51		1104.14	13376.05
1995-96	1600	7798.91	80.8	80.8	9977.7
1996-97	1760	26117.67	-	4107.82	29373.71
1997-98	2271.84	55647.32	280	2045.59	60244.76
1998-99	2928	60863.76	349.4	62071.16	65348.56
1999-00	3039	113113.2	3039	-	118135
2000-01	2550	11911	-	56234.4	65397.17
2001-02	4519.55	155644.3	-	785.5	160959.3
2002-03	7728.01	132899	-	143.25	140770.3
2003-04	34930.95	46227.09	0.02	-	81158.06
2004-05	8299	24155.3	-	-	32454.3

Source: Finance Accounts, Government of Manipur (1972-73 to 2005-06)

In order to understand the sustainability of debt of Manipur government in\terms of liquidity management i.e. ways and means advances, we need to look into ways and means and overdrafts incurred by Manipur government.

The Table 3.7 shows that the ways and means advances including special WMA and overdrafts incurred by the state. It is clear from the table that WMA including special ways and means and overdraft have been high and fluctuating. The figure which was 812.69 lakhs in 1973-74 out of the internal borrowing increased to as high as 24155.30 in 2004-05 around 29 times increase. Here, it is important to know what constitutes WMA and Overdrafts and rules and regulations. Under Section of RBI Act 1934, the RBI provides Ways and Means Advances (WMA) to the States banking with it to help them to tide over temporary mismatches in the cash flow of their receipts and payments. Such advances are under the Act, 'repayable in each case not later than three months from the date of making that advance'. There are two types of WMA; normal and special. While normal WMA are clean advances, special WMA are secured advances provided against the pledge of Government of India dated securities. The operative limit for special WMA for a State is subject to its holdings of Central Government dated securities up to a maximum of limit sanctioned. In addition, the RBI has determined limits for normal and special WMA for each State as multiples of the prescribed minimum balance required to be maintained with the RBI by that State.

Limits of WMA

The WMA limits are fixed by the Reserve Bank from time to time. Table 3.8 shows WMA limits which was effective in the past and present. However, the latest limit is based on the basis of recommendations of the Advisory Committee on Ways and Means Advances (WMA) and Overdrafts (OD) to State Governments (Chairman: Shri M.P. Bezbaruah). The new revised WMA limits for the state governments, made effective from 2006-07. Table3.8 shows WMA limits revised so far up to April1, 2006 to till date. The highest increase in percentage was 76.4 during March 1999 to January 2001 Accordingly, then aggregate Normal WMA limit was increased by 10.5 per cent to Rs. 9,875 crore for the year 2006-07.

Table 3.8
Limits of WMA

	Period	*Amount*	*Increase over earlier limits(percent)*
1	August 1996 to February 1999	2,234	Nil
2	March 1999 to January 2001	3,941	76.4
3	February 2001 to march 2002	5,283	34.1
4	April 2002 to march 2,2003	6,035	14.2
5	March 3,2003 to mach 31 2005	7,170	18.8
6	April 1,2004 to march 31 2005	8,140	13.5
7	April 1,2005 to march 31,2006	8,935	9.8
8	April1,2006 to till date	8,875	10.5

Source: RBI, study of Budget 07-08

The State-wise limits of Normal WMA were reviewed towards the end of the year. It was perceived that the extant Normal WMA limits were adequate, inter alia, on account of (i) low utilization of WMA by the State Governments during 2006-07; (ii) acclimatization of the State Governments to the changes in the fiscal environment as envisaged by the TFC, thereby signaling the end of the transition; and (iii) expected persistence of comfortable liquidity position of the State Governments during 2007-08. Accordingly, it was decided to retain the extant State-wise Normal WMA during 2007-08.

Overdraft Regulation Scheme

Any amount drawn by a State in excess of WMA is an overdraft. As per the Overdraft Regulation Scheme, in force from October 2, 1985, no State was allowed to run an overdraft with the RBI for more than seven continuous working days. In case an overdraft appeared in the State's account and remained beyond seven continuous working days, the RBI and its agencies stopped payments on behalf of the State. On a further review of the Overdraft Regulation Scheme in 1993, the time limit for clearance of overdraft was increased from seven consecutive working days to ten consecutive working days with effect from November 1, 1993.

Monitoring of WMA Overdrafts and Enforcement of Stoppage of Payments

The position of WMA actually utilized and overdrafts of various States is closely monitored in the Internal Debt Management Cell (IDM Cell), RBI, on a daily basis on receipt of the position from Central Accounts Section (CAS), RBI, Nagpur. When a State avails of WMA in excess of 75 per cent of the aggregate limit (aggregate = normal plus operative limit for special WMA), the State is cautioned to take remedial measures to avoid emergence of overdraft in its account. Whenever a State, after availing of normal and special WMA, emerges in overdraft, the IDM Cell conveys, by facsimile message, the position of its overdraft to the concerned State on a daily basis, with a request to clear a State it within a period not exceeding ten consecutive working days. If the account of te continues to be overdrawn on the eleventh continuous working day, the RBI suspends payments on behalf of the State until the overdraft is cleared.

Interest Rate on WMA and Overdrafts

The interest rate charged on WMA and overdrafts at present are the Bank Rate (9 per cent) and the Bank Rate plus two percentage points (11 per cent), respectively.

The state has been resorting to overdrafts for almost all the years under study Table 3.9. In 1976-77 the overdraft was as high as 44.65 cores. For overdrafts, the interest rates are also higher and the state has to incur extra expenditure for debt servicing. Frequently resorting to overdrafts is not a sign of prudent financial management. The Eighth Finance Commission had rightly stated that: "Unauthorized overdrafts are a sign of financial indiscipline in that concerned state government, over-spends without any regard to the availability of resources".

Table 3.9
Ways and Means Advances to Government of Manipur

(Rs. in crores)

Year	*Ways and Means Advances*	*Overdraft*	*Total*
1972-73	-	-	-
1973-74	5.90	2.23	8.13
1974-75	0.60	-	0.60
1975-76	1.62	0.77	2.39
1976-77	6.87	44.65	51.52
1977-78	7.50	17.09	24.59
1978-79	3.98	2.53	6.51
1979-80	9.39	8.56	17.95
1980-81	12.49	56.26	68.75
1981-82	5.84	116.76	122.60

Year	Ways and Means Advances	Overdraft	Total
1982-83	13.39	-27.90**	-14.51
1983-84	26.81	10.78	37.59
1984-85	48.13	21.90	70.03
1985-86	8.46	-	8.46
1986-87	-	-	-
1987-88	-	-	-
1988-89	5.02	-	5.02
1989-90	28.85	22.80	51.65
1990-91	53.31	39.91	93.22
1991-92	85.95	143.49	229.44
1992-93	61.17	204.69	265.86
1993-94	17.91	48.13	66.04
1994-95	57.84	50.13	107.97
1995-96	67.54	10.44	77.98
1996-97	144.46	1,16.72	261.18
1997-98	2,08.92	347.55	556.47
1998-99	224.13	384.50	608.60
1999-00	169.44	961.69	1131.13
2000-01	209.03	982.08	1191.11
2001-02	70.31	1486.13	1556.44
2002-03	101.54	1227.45	1328.99
2003-04	247.07	215.20	462.27
2004-05	191.24	50.31	241.55
2005-06	90.90	-	90.90

Source: Finance Accounts Government of Manipur (1972-73 to 2005-06)

There may be genuine difficulties in certain cases which to be resolved through dialogue with the Union Government but not by running into overdrafts. We are of the view that fresh liabilities should kept alignment with the availability of resources and any inescapable requirements which may arise during the year should be met by specific measures of additional resources mobilization and /or economy in expenditure. The practice to run into overdrafts is unhealthy in a federal structure like ours where, apart from a need of accelerated development, there is also an urgent needs to reduce regional disparities. Thus overdrafts are a negation of the planning process and hence should be dealt with strictly". In this context Tapan Kumar Shandilya has rightly maintained that, "The Central-state financial relationship have taken a serious turn in the late sixties due to mounting unauthorized overdrafts in the state governments with the Reserve bank of India". In this context, it is relevant to examine how many days in a year the Government of Manipur was able to maintain the minimum balances without obtaining WMA from RBI (in crores of rupees).

Table 3.10 reveals that, the no of days on which state didn't take WMA was 19 in 1981-82 reached the maximum of 306 days in 1987-88, then it had fluctuated in between 364 and 42 during 1981-82 to 2005-06, whereas in case of no of days there were shortfall from the agreed minimum balance even after having the ordinary and special WMAs to the full extent but no overdraft was taken, was at 3 in 1981-82 and reached the maximum of 143 in 1991-92, then it suddenly fell down to 8 in the next year, then it fluctuated in between 5 and 83 during the said period.

The Table 3.11 shows the average utilization of normal WMA and overdrafts by the states. All the states except Chastisgarh and Meghalaya resorted to WMA during 2001-

Table 3.10

The extent to which Manipur maintained the required minimum balances with the RBI

	1981-82	1982-83	1984-85	1985-86	1986-87	1987-88	1988-89	1989-90	1990-91	1991-92	1992-93	1993-94	1995-96	1996-97	1997-98	1998-1999	1999-2000	2000-01	2001-02	2002-03	2003-04	2004-05	2005-06
1. No of days on which the minimum balances was maintained																							
(a) without obtaining any advance	19	248	197	333	365	366	364	313	217	42	181	342	334	249	186	200	210	211	–	–	105	211	194
(b) by obtaining Ways and advances (ordinary and special)	11	30	97	32			1	34	50	84	69	8	10	65	82	83	50	45	–	45	18	13	119
2. No. of days on which there was shortfall from the agreed minimum balane even after having the ordinary and agreed minimum balane even after having the ordinary and special WMAs to the full extent but no overdraft was taken	3	–	5	–			–	–	61	143	8	1	17	7	12	7	4	1	230	30	1	16	–
3. No.of days on which overdraft was taken	332	50	66	–	–	–	–	18	37	97	107	14	34	17	85	75	102	108	135	135	212	119	44

Table 3.11

Average utilization of normal WMA and overdrafts by State governments

		2000-01	2001-02	2002-03	2003-04	2004-05	2005-06	2001-02		2002-03		2003-04		2005-06	
		No. of Days	No. of Days	No. of Days	No. of Days	No. of Days	No. of Day.s	No. of Occasion	No. of Days	No. of Occasion	No. of Days	No. of Occasion	No. of Days	No. of Occasion	No. of Days
Non-Special Category States	Andhra Pradash	336	336	72	173	0	0	24	173	6	33	6	30	0	0
	Bihar	265	265	1	92	5	0	26	123	0	0	5	44	0	0
	Goa	219	219	266	270	0	0	11	68	9	66	8	48	0	0
	Gujarat	307	307	219	203	212	0	11	72	13	47	4	21	3	13
	Haryana	299	299	64	24	116	0	16	70	4	21	0	0	0	0
	Karnataka	40	40	157	196	0	0	0	0	1	1	6	33	0	0
	Kerala	359	359	330	328	0	240	27	222	28	196	27	178	0	0
	Madhya Pradesh	290	290	251	261	7	0	15	173	22	176	10	59	0	0
	Maharastra	332	332	301	207	348	41	15	129	17	154	5	39	19	161
	Orissa	364	364	329	315	110	0	31	258	21	189	19	168	0	0
	Punjab	259	259	214	291	68	22	17	120	11	53	14	131	5	22
	Rajathan	309	309	329	303	91	0	23	169	21	151	16	94	0	6
	Tamil nadu	259	359	326	38	268	0	24	152	13	73	1	2	9	115
	Uttar Pradesh	217	217	229	321	21	34	28	83	14	79	10	100	0	0
	West Bengal	365	365	318	362	7	-	0	253	28	260	21	140	0	0
	Chhastigarh	0	0	0	0	294	0	0	0	0	0	0	0	13	98
	Jharkhand		1		31	268	0	0	0	0	0	0	0	15	115

		2000-01	2001-02	2002-03	2003-04	2004-05	2005-06	2001-02		2002-03		2003-04		2005-06	
		No. of Days	*No. of Days*	*No. of Days*	*No. of Days*	*No. of Days*	*No. of Day.s*	*No. of Occasion*	*No. of Days*	*No. of Occasion*	*No. of Days*	*No. of Occasion*	*No. of Days*	*No. of Occasion*	*No. of Days*
Special Category States	Arunachal Pradesh	13	13	27	0	35	29	0		0	0	0	0		3
	Assam	385	385	121	337	225	57	19	312	312	315	20	235	13	126
	Himachal Pradesh	342	342	252	327	159	25	29	233	233	181	14	109	4	27
	Manipur	365	365	333	268	149	63	19	331	331	350	14	201	2	118
	Meghalya	0	0	78	31	0	15	0	0	0	1	0	0	0	0
	Mizoram	270	270	184	131	147	14	10	81	81	24	3	5	1	1
	Nagaland	188	188	297	12	103	42	8	72	72	143	0	0	3	18
	Tripura	86	86	28	25	31	0	0	0	0	0	0	0	0	0
	Uttranchal	142	142	180	78	95	27	10	85	85	41	3	13		16

Source: RBI, Annual Report (200-01 to 2005-06)

02, Jharkhand resorted to WMA for only one day, the least among the Non special category states. And among the Special Category states, Assam and Manipur resorted to maximum of 365 days, Meghalya resorted to not a single day to WMA. And only three states (Chastisgarh, Jharkhand and Karnataka) availed of overdraft. In case of special category states (Arunachal Pradesh, Meghalya and Tripura) availed of overdraft in 2001-02. Although no of states availing overdraft remain the same, however, there was reduction in the no of occasions for all states.

In 2002-03, only two newly created states(Chastisgarh and Jharkhand) resorted to WMA. Regarding SCS, all the states resorted to WMA, however no of days resorting to WMA decreased to 333 in 2001-02 to 365 in 2002-03. In case of Manipur, it again decreased to 268 in 2003-04 and again decreased to 149 in 2004-05. Among the SCS only Meghalya never resorted to WMA for a single day.

In the WMA/Overdraft position of States during 2001-02 reflected continued pressure on State finances. The recourse to WMA by States during 2001-02 was generally higher than in the previous year During the year 2001-02, 20 State Governments resorted to overdrafts compared with 19 States in the previous year. While during April-July 2002, the outstanding WMAs were generally higher than those in the comparable period of the previous year, from August 2002; these have generally remained lower than the outstanding WMA in the comparable period of the previous year. The outstanding WMA and overdrafts of State Governments amounted to Rs.5, 751 crore, as on January 24, 2003 which was lower by 2.0 per cent as compared with the outstanding amount of Rs. 5,870 crore on January 25, 2002. During 2002-03, like other some states Manipur considerably reduced its recourse to WMA (in terms of no of days), however overdraft increased in terms of no of days but no of occasions remain the same in the year 2002 and 2003.

A majority of States reduced their recourse to normal WMA and overdrafts (OD) during 2003-04 (Table 3.11). The use of special WMA by the States increased by 52.7 per cent during 2003-04, mainly due to the change in provision that special WMA should be availed first before availing the normal WMA as recommended by the Ramachandran Committee (2003). The interest rate charged on Special WMA is one percentage point less than the rate on normal WMA. The buoyant proceeds from small savings and higher market borrowings (other than under the debt swap scheme) also contributed to the substantially lower recourse to the normal WMA vis-à-vis the aggregate limit of Rs.7,170 crore available for the year 2003-04. During 2003-04, some States, especially Tamil Nadu, Haryana, Nagaland and Uttaranchal considerably reduced their recourse to WMA (in terms of number of days) and overdraft (both in terms of number of days and number of occasions).

The average utilization of normal WMA, special WMA and overdrafts by the States remained substantially lower during 2005-06, reflecting an improvement in their overall cash position. VI. 26 There was a reduction in the number of States that availed normal WMA during 2005-06 (12 States as compared with 21 States in 2004-05) as well as the number of days (ranging between 14-63 days, except for Kerala which had availed normal WMA for 240 days as compared with 348 days in 2004-05). Similarly, there was a reduction in the number of the State Governments availing overdraft to overdraft on more than one occasion during the year. During 2006-07 so far (up to August 18, 2006), six

States availed of WMA for a period of 2-61 days while two States resorted to overdraft for a period ranging between 3-15 days. The lower utilization of WMA reflects persistent cash surplus with State Governments.

The daily average utilization of Normal WMA, Special WMA and overdrafts by the State Governments declined during 2006-07). During 2006-07, eight States resorted to WMA as against 12 States in the previous year. Only two States resorted to overdraft during 2006-07 as against eight States in the previous year. The lower utilization of WMA reflected improved liquidity position on the back of persistent cash surplus with the State Governments. In case of Manipur no days resorted by the government for WMA was 365 days in 2000-01. However, it gradually fell down to 149 in 2004-05and 63 in 2005-06. And in 2000-01. Manipur resorted to overdrafts for 331 days in 19 no of occasions, in 2002-03 both no of occasions and no of days increased to 331 and 350 respectively however both no of occasions and no of days gradually declined to 14 and 201 in 2003-04 and 2 and 118 in 2005-06, which is sign in the overall cash position. Here, it is quite relevant to look into the overdraft regulation and ceiling on the overdraft of government of Manipur.

Regarding, the ceiling on the Overdraft of Manipur, at the instance of Governments of Assam and Manipur, RBI has agreed to a ceiling on their overdrafts at Rs.252 crore and Rs.10 crore, respectively. If this ceiling is exceeded even within a time frame of ten consecutive working days as stipulated under the Overdraft Regulation Scheme, the RBI suspends payments on behalf of these State Governments. Therefore, from the above discussion the as it is clearly seen that, as the daily average utilization of Normal WMA,

Special WMA and overdrafts by the State Governments declined during 2006-07. No of days and no of occasions of overdrafts resorted by government of Manipur are seen to be gradually declining in the past five years. It signifies a sign of financial discipline in the Manipur and availability of resources and improvement in the overall cash position of the state government.

CHAPTER 4

BURDEN OF PUBLIC DEBT

The nature and extent of public debt depend on many factors, such as the purpose for which loan is advanced, their terms and conditions, their structure and the maturity mix, their types and rate of interest, the debt management policy and the general economic and social conditions of the state. New ideas and concepts have emerged in the analysis of public debt as discussed in the previous chapters. Most of the analysis in public finance literature of the growth and of inter-governmental loans have been confined to central debt. The problems arising from the increasing burden of the state government has not been seriously examined. Therefore, growing magnitude of debt problems accompanied by new dimension of burden of debt of the state government call for a fresh look into the specific state. A clear idea about the burden of the public debt would be useful to build up a theoretical base for analyzing the impact of central loans on the economy of the state. A brief discussion on the theories of the burden of Public debt will be relevant and these theories will be used to study the impact of intergovernmental loans.

The Concept of Burden

The concept of the burden of public debt is an extremely vague one. Generally, a distinction may be drawn between financial burden and real burden or secondary burden. When a debt is obtained by the government, the level of taxation in the economy has to be increased in order to meet the interest change so long as the debt continues to exist. To the extent of the increase in the tax level, the income of the people is transferred to the government. The consequent loss in the income of the people may be called financial burden of public debt. David M.C. Wright rightly observes, "The financial burden of the national debt is to be measured by the effects of the interest changes and the taxes levied to meet them. The relation which the taxes for interest bear to the national money income is the question of primary importance".

When a debt is obtained by the government, the financial burden may be defined as the loss in income of the people that aims on account of taxation for meeting the servicing cost of the debt. The concept of burden is sometimes explained in terms of the taxation explained in terms of the notion of abstinence or pain-cost doctrine and opportunity cost. When a loan is raised by the government, resources are transferred from private hands to government and those who contribute to government loans abstain from current income and undergo the pain of abstinence which may be called a burden caused by incurring of public debt. Similarly on the basis of the principle of opportunity cost, it is said that public debt entails a burden because, when a loan is raised by the government, people are prevented from putting their resources into other purposes, the marginal productivity of which might be more. But the concept of burden based on the notion of abstinence and opportunity cost is not acceptable, if people contribute to public loans voluntarily.

When people voluntarily lend to the government, it means by investing in government securities, they are moving to a preferred position on the utility surface. The secondary burden of the debt may emerge on account of the adverse effects of taxation upon the ability and willingness to work and on the capacity and willingness to save. This may be termed as the real burden of the public debt.

The Burden Controversy

The burden controversy is one of the oldest subjects of academic discussions since the days of Mercantilism. After the Keynesian Revolution the controversy had reached its logical conclusion. However, in the 1960s, it seemed that this issue had attained its logical end but in 1958, the Publication of James M. Buchanan's treatise, "Public Principles of Public Debt," the controversy again became lively as both economists and politicians came out with highly controversial views regarding the burden of public debt. Being aware of limitations of the theories of Prof. Buchanan, a modified version of Buchanan thesis of transferability of the burden of public debt is presented by three American Economists William G. Bown, Richard G. Davis and David H. Kopf (BDK). BDK adopt two different definitions of the burden of public debt and say that in one case the burden is not transferable and in other case the burden is transferable. If the real burden of a debt to a generation is defined as the total consumption as a consequence of government borrowing and attendant public spending it may be argued that burden will be shifted to future generations. What emerges from the foregoing discussion of the burden of public debt is that debt is neither an evil nor a blessing in itself. It has both adverse effects and favorable effects on the state finance. It is an instrument of public policy, but it is one which should be used with care.

Here, we may point out that in the case of state's debt to central government there can never be any direct money burden as we are dealing with debtors and creditors of the same country. If there is at all any burden or benefit it is real as Dalton observes, "The debt will involve a direct real burden or a direct real benefit to the community according to the nature of the series of transfers from the tax payer to the tax public creditors. Primarily it will bring burden or benefit, according as the transfers increase or decrease the inequality of income". Thus, it is clear that the financial impact of central loans on state refers to the amount of debt servicing charges, i.e. interest charges and repayment of the loans. Such type of financial burden falls both on the revenue and the capital accounts of the budgets.

The interest charges and its non-development expenditure of the revenue account and repayments are capital disbursements of the capital account. In view of this discussion, the financial effects can be classified as: (1) Income effects, and (2) Substitution effects. The former relate to the financial transfer from the state budget to the central budget in shape of debt servicing charges, i.e. interest charge and repayments, therefore, the income effects of financial impacts of central loans on the state maybe measured, as referred above, in the form of: (a) the percentage of interest charges to the total revenue, the total tax revenue and total revenue expenditure (b) the percentage of repayments to total capital receipts and capital disbursements, (c) the percentage of interest and repayment charges to total revenue expenditure, total debt, total gross loans and total net domestic product. The substitution effects relate to the impact of union loans on the revenue mobilizing efforts of the state.

In order to know the long term economic effects of the loan on the economy of the state, it is important to look into whether the loans are used for productive or unproductive purposes, whether capital formation and income generation are not adversely affected. In this context the financial impact of central loans on the state is examined in order to know effects of central loans on the state economy. As discussed earlier, it refers to the amount of interest charges and repayments which are paid annually and which are imposed on the budget of the state. As before, financial impact has been classified into income effects and substitution effects. The former refers to the annual flow of resources from the state to the centre government on account of debt repayments and interest charges. The latter refers to the states' failure to mobilize financial resources in adequate amount because financial assistance is readily available from the central government. The income effects of the financial burden/ impact may be measured, as pointed out earlier, in terms of the percent of interest charges to states' total revenue, total tax to total state's tax revenue, total capital receipts, total capital disbursements and the percentage of interest charges and repayments to states' total revenue, total tax revenue and total revenue expenditure.

From the foregoing chapters, it is concluded that central loans have emerged as the most important component of the total debt of the state and growth of debt servicing charges has been influenced by it. The interest charges on central loans increased from 3.27 crores in 1980-81 to Rs. 125.06 crores in 2005-06 under the study (Table 4.1). It means that it increased by more than 38 times during this period. The repayment of central loans has been fluctuating during the period, it reached the lowest at Rs 3.86 cores in 1983-84 and reached the maximum of Rs. 599.26 crores in 2003-04, then fell down to 43.33 crores in 2005-06.

Table 4.1
Financial Burden of Central Loans on the Revenue Budget of Manipur (Crores)

Year	*States total tax revenue (Crores)*	*States total Revenue (Crores)*	*States total revenue expenditure (Crores)*	*Interest Charges on central loans (Crores)*	*Repayment of Central Loans (Crores)*	*5+6*	*7 as percent of 2*	*7 as percent of 4*	*7 as percent of 3*
1	2	3	4	5	6	7			
1980-81	4.45	110.94	69.79	3.27	54.04	57.31	1287.87	82.12	51.66
1981-82	5.81	95.08	85.12	2.22	22.48	24.7	425.13	29.02	25.98
1982-83	6.27	116.63	92.63	2.38	5.97	8.35	133.17	9.01	7.16
1983-84	6.95	129.68	105.99	2.06	3.86	5.92	85.18	5.59	4.57
1984-85	8.84	171.38	133.76	7.8	10.97	18.77	212.33	14.03	10.95
1985-86	11.08	226.27	155.83	6.18	25.66	31.84	287.36	20.43	14.07
1986-87	14.07	248.32	198.06	9.52	17.15	26.67	189.55	13.47	10.74
1987-88	16.63	286.53	214.59	13.27	12.61	25.88	155.62	12.06	9.03
1988-89	18	523.25	279.07	7.53	13.21	20.74	115.22	7.43	3.96
1989-90	20.23	334.19	334.19	11.06	16.47	27.53	136.09	8.24	8.24
1990-91	19.51	390.19	390.19	12.89	22.87	35.76	183.29	9.16	9.16
1991-92	22.56	435.2	384.51	15.18	44.13	59.31	253.5	15.51	13.21
1992-93	25.6	480.22	378.84	17.48	65.39	82.87	323.71	21.87	17.26
1993-94	32.12	567.92	438.02	18.13	72.78	90.91	283.03	20.75	16.01
1994-95	39.09	592.08	508.34	17.33	17.24	34.57	88.44	6.8	5.84

Year	States total tax revenue (Crores)	States total Revenue (Crores)	States total revenue expenditure (Crores)	Interest Charges on central loans (Crores)	Repayment of Central Loans (Crores)	5+6	7 as percent of 2	7 as percent of 4	7 as percent of 3
1995-96	59.32	691.68	618.77	17.82	10.13	27.95	47.12	4.52	4.04
1996-97	69.36	822.9	710.31	21	33.72	54.72	78.89	7.7	6.65
1997-98	95.24	863.01	790.77	48.11	74.66	122.77	128.91	15.53	14.23
1998-99	71.62	896.78	1347.99	33.21	98.59	131.8	184.03	9.78	14.7
1999-00	78.45	1069.85	1123.44	39.55	28.94	68.49	87.3	6.1	6.4
2000-01	60.89	1044.62	1337.96	48.22	87.1	135.32	222.24	10.11	12.95
2001-02	193.15	1176.78	1415.11	70.37	592.49	662.86	343.18	46.84	56.33
2002-03	253.28	1327.99	1415.11	124.75	577.85	702.6	277.4	49.65	52.91
2003-04	309.13	1419.71	1463.47	124.56	599.26	723.82	234.15	49.46	50.98
2004-05	368.41	1742.76	1651.19	109.04	382.2	491.24	133.34	29.75	28.19
2005-06	437.09	2408.95	2004.51	125.06	43.33	168.39	38.53	8.40	6..99

Source: Finance Accounts Government of Manipur (1980-81 to 2005-06)

Table 4.2
The financial burden of union Loans on the state (Interest charges on Union Loans as percent of states tax revenue, Total Revenue and state Revenue Expenditure) of Manipur

(crores of Rupees)

Year	*Interest charges on Union Loans (crores)*	*Interest charges as percent of*		
		States' tax revenue	*State's total revenue*	*State's revenue expenditure*
1980-81	5	73.53	2.95	7.16
1981-82	3.27	38.27	2.34	3.84
1982-83	2.22	38.07	2.05	2.4
1983-84	2.38	29.64	1.59	2.25
1984-85	2.06	88.38	4.56	1.54
1985-86	7.8	55.8	2.73	5.01
1986-87	6.18	67.73	3.84	3.12
1987-88	9.52	79.82	4.63	4.44
1988-89	13.27	41.83	1.44	4.76
1989-90	7.53	54.71	3.31	2.25
1990-91	11.06	66.08	3.3	2.83
1991-92	15.18	67.18	3.95	3.11
1992-93	12.89	68.28	4.61	3.4
1993-94	17.48	56.45	4.14	3.99
1994-95	18.13	44.33	3.41	3.57
1995-96	17.33	30.05	2.88	2.8
1996-97	17.82	30.28	2.96	2.51
1997-98	21	50.52	6.08	2.66
1998-99	48.11	46.37	2.46	35.69
1999-00	33.21	50.42	3.52	2.96
2000-01	39.55	79.2	3.6	2.96
2001-02	48.22	36.44	4.97	3.41
2002-03	70.37	49.26	8.82	4.97
2003-04	124.75	40.29	8.51	8.52
2004-05	124.56	29.6	6.6	7.54
2005-06	109.04	28.61	6.24	5.44

Source: Derived from Finance Accounts, Government of Manipur (1980-81 to 2005-06)

Table 4.2, highlights the total income effect of the financial burden of central loans of the state. It also indicates the total financial burden by adding the interest charges and repayment, it also demonstrates the total income effects by relating both interest charges and debt repayments to the total state revenue, total tax revenue and total revenue expenditure of the state.

It is also clear from Table 4.2 that proportion of interest charges and debt repayment to the total tax revenue was 1287.87, which was the highest in 1980-81. Since then it has fluctuated in between 3.8 percent and 425.13 percent during the study period. The interest charges and debt repayment as a proportion of the total revenue of the state was highest in 1980-81 when it was 51.66, then it fell down gradually to reach 4.57 in 1983-84, since then it has fluctuated in between 3.96 and 56.33.

The percentage of interest charge and debt repayment of revenue expenditure was highest in 1980 81 when it was 82.12 and it has fluctuated around 49.65 and 4.52 percent. The debt servicing charges are charges on the state tax revenue. Being a charge on the tax revenue, it becomes a burden on the economy as it adversely affects the rte of capital formation. The growth of debt servicing charges has been as is clear form table (4.2) above, spectacular but thus need not have caused much anxiety, if the borrowed funds had been spent on entirely on productive capital investments and the investments would have been able to meet the repayment liability and debt servicing charges. But as had been the case, the investments made so far had generally proved to be un-remunerative and so the repayment of debt incurred, had placed heavy burden on the states finances.

It is clear from the Table 4.2 that interest charges on central loans have been increasing very consistently in absolute terms from 190-81 to 2005-06. The impact of public debt depends not only on its size but upon the rate of interest and amortization i.e. the total amount of interest and payment of principal that falls due to be paid in particular year. Sound principle of public debt management warrants minimization of servicing cost, so the impact/burden of state's central loans should be judged not only on the basis of their magnitude but on the basis of the servicing cost. There is generally a functional relationship between the magnitude of the public debt and cost of servicing debt with increasing debt (increasing both absolutely and relatively), servicing cost of the debt have been increasing, which is clear from the Table 4.2 indicates that the percentage of interest charges to states' total tax revenue was 73.53 in 1980-81, fell down to 38.27 in the next succeeding year, continued to decline to 29.64 in 1983-84 and rose abruptly to 88.38 in 1984-85, it is seen that, the percentage of interest charges to states' total tax revenue have been fluctuating and gradually it started declining from 2002-03 and it fell down to lowest at 28.61 in 2005-06. It signifies that a very significant part of states' tax revenue went back to the centre in the form of interest charges, however it started to improve after 2002-03. It also shows that a very significant part of the state's tax revenue went back to the centre in the form of interest charges but in the recent years it showed a slight improvement. Table 4.2 shows that the percentage of interest charges on central loans to total state revenue was 2.95 in 1980-81, it went on decreasing till 1983-84 and started rising, and reached the maximum of 9.39 percent in 2002-03. It is clear that income effect of thee financial burden of interest charges on central loans has been fluctuating and in some years it was below 3 percent and the magnitude of the percentage was also small. This is due to the debt relief given by the Finance commission. The above tables also indicates that interest charges as a proportion of the states revenue expenditure has been fluctuating, it was 4.09 percent in 1980-81 and declined to 1.94 percent in 1983-84 then it started rising absolutely from 1990 till 2005-06.

The Table 4.3 provides the increasing income effect of the financial burden/impact of the repayment of central loans, which has its bad effects on the capital budgets of the state. The amount of repayments shows a high fluctuating trend. It has increased from 54.4 Crores to reach a maximum amount of Rs 599.26 in 2003-04. It feel down gradually to 43.3 in 2005-06. It is also clear from the table that proportion of repayment of central Loans to the capital disbursement of the state was 160.77, which was the maximum ratio, and in the following years it gradually started to decrease to reach the minimum of 0.27, since then it has been fluctuating and reach the maximum value of 785.17 in 2001-02, then gradually declined to reach as low as 7.04 in 200506. The proportion of repayment as proportion of in 1986-87, in the next year it rose to 5.71, since then it has been fluctuating 1.92 and 30.74. The proportion of repayment as proportion of gross loan from the centre was 128.45 in 1980-81 declined to 7.74 in 1982-83, since then it has been fluctuating and it reach as high as 1448.28 in 2000-01, then it started declining to reach 4.58 in 2005-06. And repayment as proportion of total outstanding debt was 47.09 in 1980-81 declined in the following years to reach 7.06 in 1983-84 then it rose to reach the maximum value of 59.26 in 1986-87, then it fluctuated in the following years to reach 6.40 in 2005-06.

Table 4.3
The financial burden of Union loans on the Capital Budget of the state, Manipur

(in crores of rupees)

Years	Repayment of Central Loans	Capital disbursements	Column 2 as % Column 3	Column 2 as % of Gross loan from the centre	Column 2 as % of total debt of the state
1980-81	54.05	33.62	160.77	128.45	47.09
1981-82	22.49	35.61	63.16	102.23	15.18
1982-83	5.97	38.15	15.65	7.74	8.93
1983-84	0.14	51.77	0.27	31.18	7.06
1984-85	10.92	50.63	21.57	107.87	11.94
1985-86	25.67	60.64	42.33	59.76	41.47
1986-87	17.15	779.07	2.2	101.72	59.26
1987-88	12.61	86.08	14.65	95.97	49.86
1988-89	13.21	100.53	13.14	71.29	31.89
1989-90	16.47	104.09	15.82	59.98	17.66
1990-91	22.88	127.59	17.93	40.07	12.22
1991-92	44.38	113.66	42	223.74	14.59
1992-93	65.89	99.73	66.07	407.41	16.96
1993-94	72.78	118.93	61.2	125.27	35.76
1994-95	17.24	144.91	11.9	23.75	8.77
1995-96	10.13	175.2	5.78	44.26	6.4
1996-97	33.72	262.55	12.84	161.88	8.12
1997-98	74.66	254.56	29.33	175.26	9.46
1998-99	98.59	214.25	46.02	73.96	11.56
1999-00	28.94	363.76	7.96	10.69	1.8
2000-01	87.1	147.49	59.05	98.84	5.36
2001-02	592.49	75.46	785.17	1448.28	26.23
2002-03	577.85	160.7	359.58	811.7	22.65
2003-04	599.26	240.39	249.29	58.47	41.04
2004-05	382.2	521.18	73.33	448.17	25.2
2005-06	43.33	615.82	7.04	4.58	6.4

Source: Finance Accounts, Government of Manipur

It is also clear that the amount of repayments of central loans has been higher than that of the interest charges. It implies that Manipur is facing considerable strain on its capital budget.

Table 4.4
Financial burden of Union Loans on the Budget of the Manipur (Interest and Repayment of Union Loans as percent of total tax revenue total revenue and total revenue expenditure of the state)

Years	*Interest on Union and Repayment (Crores)*	*Interest on Union and Repayment as % of revenue expenditure*		
1980-81	57.32	1288.09	51.67	82.13
1981-82	24.71	425.3	25.99	29.03
1982-83	8.35	133.17	7.16	9.01
1983-84	2.2	31.65	1.7	2.08
1984-85	18.72	211.76	10.92	14
1985-86	31.85	287.45	14.08	20.41
1986-87	26.67	189.55	10.74	13.47
1987-88	25.88	155.53	9.03	12.06
1988-89	20.74	115.22	3.96	7.43
1989-90	27.53	136.09	8.24	8.24
1990-91	35.77	183.34	0.09	9.17
1991-92	59.57	254.5	8.72	15.59
1992-93	83.37	325.66	17.36	22.01
1993-94	90.91	283.03	16.01	20.75
1994-95	34.57	88.41	5.84	6.8
1995-96	27.95	47.11	4.04	4.52
1996-97	54.72	78.89	6.65	7.7

Years	*Interest on Union and Repayment (Crores)*	*Interest on Union and Repayment as % of revenue expenditure*		
1997-98	122.77	128.91	14.23	15.53
1998-99	131.8	184.03	14.7	97.78
1999-00	68.49	87.3	6.4	6.1
2000-01	135.32	222.24	12.95	10.11
2001-02	662.86	343.18	56.33	46.84
2002-03	702.6	277.4	52.91	49.65
2003-04	723.82	234.16	512.66	49.46
2004-05	491.24	133.34	28.17	29.75
2005-06	168.39	38.52	69.89	8.4

Source: Same as Table 4.3

Table 4.4 shows that the percentage of interest charge and debt repayment of revenue expenditure was highest in 1980-81 when it was 82.12 and it has fluctuated around 49.65 and 4.52 percent. The debt servicing charges are charges on the state tax revenue. Being a charge on the tax revenue, it becomes a burden on the economy as it adversely affects the rte of capital formation. The growth of debt servicing charges has been as is clear from Table 4.3 above, spectacular but thus need not have caused much anxiety, if the borrowed funds had been spent on entirely on productive capital investments and the investments would have been able to meet the repayment liability and debt servicing charges. But as had been the case, the investments made so far had generally proved to be un-remunerative and so the repayment of debt incurred, had placed heavy burden on the states finances.

Table 4.5
Financial Burden of internal debt of Manipur

Year	*Interest on internal debt (Crores)*	*Repayment of internal Debt (Crores)*	*Column 2 + colmn3*	*Column 4 as % of Total tax revenue*	*Column 4 as % of Total revenue Expenditure*
1980-81		64.59	65.84	1479.55	59.35
1981-82	0.61	77.7	78.31	1347.85	82.36
1982-83	0.51	37.21	37.72	601.59	32.34
1983-84	2.06	28.1	30.16	433.96	23.26
1984-85	2.68	73.3	75.98	859.5	44.33
1985-86	3.78	17.51	21.29	192.15	9.41
1986-87	4.76	8.21	12.97	92.18	5.22
1987-88	3.29	2.26	5.55	33.35	1.94
1988-89	7.09	7.71	14.8	82.22	2.83
1989-90	7.65	42.75	50.4	249.13	15.08
1990-91	11.14	98.55	109.69	562.22	0.28
1991-92	13.56	194.19	207.75	878.41	31.98
1992-93	15.98	289.84	305.82	1194.61	63.68
1993-94	19.56	81.83	101.39	315.66	17.85
1994-95	13.19	110.43	123.62	316.16	20.88
1995-96	14.91	60.68	75.59	127.41	10.93
1996-97	28.82	221.05	249.87	360.25	30.36
1997-98	17.54	415.11	432.65	454.27	50.13
1998-99	38.58	424.49	463.07	646.57	51.64
1999-00	58.07	1261.6	1319.67	1682.18	123.35
2000-01	76.94	1068.28	1145.22	1880.8	109.63
2001-02	70.92	1465.32	1536.24	795.36	130.55
2002-03	85.11	1765.98	1851.09	730.85	139.39
2003-04	54.94	650.98	705.92	228.36	499.98
2004-05	121.48	315.94	437.42	118.73	25.09
2005-06	73.73	164.39	238.12	54.48	98.83

Source: same as Table 4.4

Table 4.6
Outstanding debt as percentage of NSDP of Manipur

Year	*Outstanding Central Loans (in Crores)*	*NSDP (in Crores)*	*Column. 2 as percent col. 3*
1980-81	45.21	199.56	22.65
1981-82	44.72	242.02	18.48
1982-83	115.79	256.35	45.17
1983-84	124.31	303.98	40.89
1984-85	123.51	344.49	35.85
1985-86	140.78	372.25	37.82
1986-87	140.49	426.04	32.98
1987-88	141.02	541.77	26.03
1988-89	146.34	605.83	24.16
1989-90	157.34	634.08	24.81
1990-91	191.55	723.01	26.49
1991-92	184.39	867.69	21.25
1992-93	177.1	957.11	18.5
1993-94	176.9	1156.97	15.29
1994-95	182.56	1305.97	13.98
1995-96	196.01	1412.23	13.88
1996-97	227.7	1510.65	15.07
1997-98	286.34	1881.51	15.22
1998-99	334.9	2125.21	15.76
1999-00	398.83	2954.11	13.5
2000-01	548.64	2954.11	18.57
2001-02	460.35	2813.64	16.36
2002-03	907.44	3014.08	30.11
2003-04	835.49	3141.73	26.59
2004-05	1480.5	3564.35	41.54
2005-06	1442.24	5454.06	26.44

Note: percentage have been calculated.

Source: 1. *Outstanding Central Loans to State: Finance account, Government of Manipur (1980-2005)*

2. *State's NSDP: Statistical Abstracts (various issues)*

As the increasing central loans as percentage of state domestic product are feared because they may ultimately lead to higher taxes for servicing the debt. Therefore, in order to understand the impact of central loans on state domestic product, the ratio of the central loans to state domestic product may be measured. Hence, let us examine the relation between outstanding central Loans and state net domestic product. It is an important indicator of manageability or otherwise of central loans in the state. The impact has been shown in the Table 4.6. The economic development impact relates to the position and growth of state income vis-à-vis debt servicing charges. The impact has been shown in the Table 4.7

It is clear from the Table 4.7 that interest charge as proportion of net Domestic product was 1.65, sarted declined to reach minimum of 0.68 and in the next year it went up to 2.27. But, thereafter, it shows the fluctuating trend during the following year and fluctuated very marginally and reached the maximum of 3.96 in 2003-04. The position of repayment as proportion of Net State domestic Product was somewhat different. There was no steady trend. Repayment of central loans as proportion of Net State domestic Product, which was 27.08 declined to 9.28 in the following year next year to reach the minimum of 0.05 in 1983-84, then it raised to 19.17 in 2002-03, thereafter it showed a declining trend in the following year to as low as 0.79 in 2005-06. The table also indicates the same trend in case of the proportion of interest and repayments to State's NSDP. The above findings are disturbing.

It would be reasonable to conclude that that the burden of large public debt is not a decisive obstacle to economic growth. Certainly the debt income ratio is very small. But, our state being a poor state. Even this percentage matters

Table 4.7
Economic Development impact Central Loans on the Manipur

(in Crores of Rupees)

Years	*Interest Charges on Central Loans*	*Repayment of Central Loans*	*Interest and Repayment of Central loans*	*NSDP*	*Column 2 as percent of column 5*	*Column 3 as percent column 5*	*Column 4 as Percent of column 5*
1980-81	3.27	54.05	57.32	199.56	1.64	27.08	28.72
1981-82	2.22	22.49	24.71	242.02	0.92	9.29	10.21
1982-83	2.39	5.97	8.36	256.35	0.93	2.33	3.26
1983-84	2.06	0.14	2.2	303.98	0.68	0.05	0.72
1984-85	7.81	10.92	18.73	344.49	2.27	3.17	5.44
1985-86	6.18	25.67	31.85	372.25	1.66	6.9	8.56
1986-87	9.53	17.15	26.68	426.04	2.24	4.03	6.26
1987-88	13.28	12.61	25.89	541.77	2.45	2.33	4.78
1988-89	7.53	13.21	20.74	605.83	1.24	2.18	3.42
1989-90	11.07	16.47	27.54	634.08	1.75	2.6	4.34
1990-91	12.89	22.88	35.77	723.01	1.78	3.16	4.95
1991-92	15.18	44.38	59.57	840.06	1.8	5.02	6.83
1992-93	17.48	65.89	83.37	957.11	1.83	6.88	8.71

Years	Interest Charges on Central Loans	Repayment of Central Loans	Interest and Repayment of Central loans	NSDP	Column 2 as percent of column 5	Column 3 as percent column 5	Column 4 as Percent of column 5
1993-94	18.13	72.78	90.91	1156.97	1.57	6.29	7.86
1994-95	17.33	17.24	34.57	1305.97	1.33	1.32	2.65
1995-96	17.83	10.13	27.96	1412.23	1.26	0.72	1.98
1996-97	21	33.72	54.72	1510.65	1.39	2.23	3.62
1997-98	48.11	74.66	122.77	1881.51	2.56	3.97	6.53
1998-99	33.21	98.59	131.8	2125.21	1.56	4.64	6.2
1999-00	39.55	28.94	68.49	2954.11	1.34	0.98	2.32
2000-01	48.22	87.1	135.32	2954.11	1.63	2.95	4.58
2001-02	70.37	592.49	662.86	2813.64	2.5	21.06	23.56
2002-03	124.76	577.85	702.61	3014.08	4.14	19.17	23.31
2003-04	124.56	599.26	723.82	3141.73	3.96	19.07	23.04
2004-05	109.04	382.2	491.24	3564.35	3.06	10.72	13.78
2005-06	125.07	43.33	168.4	5454.06	2.29	0.79	3.09

Source: same as that of Table no 4.6

much because the capability of the state to bear the burden is low and therefore the impact of central loan may be adverse on the economy.

The problem may be examined from other point of view i.e. rate of growth of state domestic product. If the rate of growth of central loans is greater than the rate of NSDP, it may be considered a symptomatic of bad financial affairs in the long period. In the short period i.e., in initial sate of economic development especially in the plan economy, the rate of growth of NSDP, because of government's heavy investment in social and economic infrastructure and key and heavy industries having long gestation periods. Therefore, the main problem is the low rate of growth of state income rather than increase the rapid increase in the debt. Thus the problem of 'debt servicing burden' becomes a problem of increasing national income. It is absolutely necessary to speed up the rate of growth of the economy from the point of making the burden of debt-servicing less onerous. If the targeted rate of growth of the economy cannot be achieved the growing debt imposes in heavy strain on the economy. In the long run, the growth of income might be faster. But in an economy like ours where the lake of supply of commodities is causing inflationary rise in prices, the burden, even in the short run, may not be overlooked. But still this ratio does not give any clear picture of the burden of the central loan because it is just possible that increase in the state's income is not due to the effective utilization of borrowed sum but on account of certain other factors. However, we have the 'link relations' of the central loans and state income separately and on their basis we can examine and compare their rate of growth.

Table 4.8
Comparative studies of the rate of growth of Central Loans and NSDP of Manipur

Years	*Link growth of Outstanding debt*	*Link growth of NSDP*
1980-81	101.1	82.46
1981-82	38.62	94.41
1982-83	93.15	84.33
1983-84	100.65	88.24
1984-85	87.73	92.54
1985-86	100.21	87.37
1986-87	99.62	78.64
1987-88	96.36	89.43
1988-89	93.01	95.54
1989-90	82.14	87.7
1990-91	103.88	83.33
1991-92	104.12	90.66
1992-93	100.11	82.73
1993-94	96.9	88.59
1994-95	93.14	92.48
1995-96	86.08	93.48
1996-97	79.52	80.29
1997-98	85.5	88.53
1998-99	83.97	71.94
1999-00	72.69	100
2000-01	119.18	104.99
2001-02	50.73	93.35
2002-03	108.61	95.94
2003-04	56.43	88.14
2004-05	102.65	65.35

Source: 1. *Outstanding Central Loans to Sate-Finance account, Government of Manipur (1980-2005)*

2. *State's NSDP-Statistical Abstracts (various issues)*

The link Relatives have been calculated as calculated by Shandhalya Method of calculation of Link Relatives:

$$\text{Link relatives} = \frac{\text{Current year data}}{\text{Previous year data}} \times 100$$

It is clear from Table 4.8 that the rate of growth of central loans and that of state's net domestic product are almost steady. The rate of growth of outstanding central loans were more than that of that of NSDP in the following years, in 1980-81, 82-83, 83-84, 85-86 to 88, 1990-91, 1994-95, 1998-99, 2000-01, 2002-03. This is certainly bad. The principle of sound finance requires that the rate of growth of central loans should be less than the rate growth of SDP.

The measure is based upon the reasoning that the burden of the loan should not be judged on the basis of volume or size but on the basis of its impact upon the productivity in the economy. If with the increasing volume of the debt, NSDP is increasing satisfactorily, the debt may entail any burden or not will spend upon the rate of increase in NSDP. MCC Wright maintains that even though interest charges and consequent tax frictions are rising absolutely, the relative tax friction may be decreasing, if the national money and real income is increasing at faster rate. Thus, if we have genuine growths in taxable capacity continues to grow as fast, faster than the taxes.

The impact of central loans can be analyzed from one more angle. It would be purposeful to assess the incidence of central loans in relation to growth in aggregate expenditure also apart from growth in income which has already been discussed. This, indeed, was also approach of the eighth Finance Commission which had a special term of reference to examine the State's non plan capital gaps. Table 4.9 relates to the burden of debt repayment and servicing to the state's aggregate expenditure (revenue + capital). It may be observed from the table that the burden of debt-repayment and servicing started to increased abruptly from 2000-01 and it had almost the same in the subsequent three years but it fell down to 6.43 percent in 2005-06.

T. Shandilya has rightly observed that it is capital formation in the public sector which is the true indicator of the burden, or otherwise of central Loans. But, in the case of Manipur, most of the Public sector Undertakings out of 18 PSUs in the state have become unviable and are not in a position to yield any returns.

Table 4.9
Burden of debt repayment and servicing to the state's aggregate expenditure (revenue + capital)

Years	*Aggregate Expenditure*	*Repayment + Interest to Centre*	*Column 3 as percent of column2*
1980-81	103.41	57.32	55.43
1981-82	120.73	24.71	20.47
1982-83	130.78	8.35	6.38
1983-84	157.76	2.2	1.39
1984-85	184.39	18.72	10.15
1985-86	216.47	31.85	14.71
1986-87	977.13	26.67	2.73
1987-88	300.67	25.88	8.61
1988-89	379.6	20.74	5.46
1989-90	438.28	27.53	6.28
1990-91	517.78	35.77	6.91
1991-92	498.28	59.57	12.16
1992-93	478.57	83.37	17.42

Years	*Aggregate Expenditure*	*Repayment + Interest to Centre*	*Column 3 as percent of column2*
1993-94	556.95	90.91	16.32
1994-95	653.25	34.57	5.29
1995-96	793.97	27.95	3.52
1996-97	972.86	54.72	5.62
1997-98	1045.33	122.77	11.74
1998-99	1562.24	131.8	8.44
1999-00	1487.2	68.49	4.61
2000-01	1485.45	135.32	9.11
2001-02	1490.57	662.86	44.47
2002-03	1575.81	702.6	44.59
2003-04	1703.86	723.82	42.48
2004-05	2172.37	491.24	22.61
2005-06	2620.33	168.39	6.43

Note: Aggregate Expenditure = Revenue Expenditure + Capital Expenditure

Source: Interest and repayment of Union Loans:

Net Domestic Product various issues of Statistical Abstract

This shows that economic development burden has increased year after year. This is indicative of the extent of misutilisation of the central Loans to the state in the name of capital expenditure. The central Loans are not accompanied by the increase in the rate of asset creation. If the borrowed funds are used for asset creating public projects, the income of the state is bound to increase. The cost of the burden would be then off set by the benefits that the debt-creation confers. However, at least the part of the rise in state income may be attributed to the rise in central loans which provided funds for public investment. Tax revenue is mostly utilized for the normal expenditure of the Government and therefore, for financing economic development of the state, there is heavy reliance on finances borrowed from the centre. In this context, it is quite important to look into the utilization of the Loan. As the utilization part is certainly more significant because it is neither the volume of the central loans nor the magnitude of debt servicing charges that determines the burden. If the central Loans and debt service charges are increasing rapidly but simultaneously if the assets are also increasing in the economy, the impact of the loans will be duly off set by the benefits deserve from the loans. No doubt, the rising central loans have certainly contributed to the increase in the states income because volume of investment in the five year plans would have bee what is without central loans. Therefore, at least the part of the rise in state's income may be attributed to the rise in central loans which provided funds for public investments. Here, it is quite important to look into the utilization part as utilizations is certainly more significant because it is neither the volume of the central loan nor the magnitude of the debt servicing charges that determine the burden. If the Central loans and debt servicing charges are increasing rapidly but simultaneously if the assets are increased, the impact of the loan will be duly off set by the benefits deserved from loans.

CHAPTER 5

SOCIAL DEVELOPMENT IMPACT OF PUBLIC DEBT MANAGEMENT

The current debt management strategy is based on a firm view on the point of national perspective that debt management is good for the debted states. Public debt management in the short run provides a basis for long term growth in the future and structural adjustment offer the best hope for realizing development in Human and Social development in the economy. The issue of positive or negative impact of public debt management in achieving the macro economic objectives has been frequently discussed. Some Economist argue that at best, these programmes do little in the way of improving economic indicators while others have gone so far as to say that programmers worsen the situation. Emphasis on the growth rate of the macro economic variables has over the years been accepted as the yardstick of progress of a nation. Here, an important fact that needs to be noted is that, "with bulk of the responsibilities pertaining to expenditure on social sectors placed in the domain of the state governments, it is widely recognized that the level of social sector expenditure has important implications for the level of human development and long term prospects of the economy. Consequently, while the union government may be keen on minimizing the social costs of economic reforms, the actual outcome in this sphere depends on the actions taken by the numerous state governments. Indian states differ a great deal from one another in terms of level of social attainment as well as government policies pertaining to them. Given such a variegated picture, it is quite relevant that impact of social expenditure on human and social development will differ across the states. Consequently, it is necessary that studies seeking to understand the impact on social sectors from any government policy should focus their attention on the experience of specific states. In the light of the above discussion, a question that is frequently raised in connection with public debt management is whether the government has been effective in achieving a positive impact on social and human development in the state. Therefore, in this chapter, an attempt is made to study the impact of public debt management on human and development. However, before proceeding further, it is necessary to clarify the terms used in the study on account of their numerous connotations.

Social Sector

The term social sector is often used to refer to Education, Health and Nutrition sectors. The term hasn't been defined formally defined and thus has come to acquire several connotations. Two main approaches to the definition may be identified: one views social sectors from a Human Resource Development point of view; the other takes the Human Development Approach. In what follows I attempt an examination of these two approaches to the analysis of social sectors.

The Human Resource Development Approach

The human Resource Development Approach emphasizes investment in Education, health and nutrition as a means of enhancing the quality of human capital which may be defined as "the stock of skills and productive knowledge embodied in people". The human capital approach attracted attention during the 1960s when Schultz (1961) and Becker (1962) highlighted the viewpoint that education, health and nutrition cannot be considered merely as consumption goods.

The expenditure on schooling, health, on-the-job training, and searching for information about job opportunities and migration constitutes an investment that people make in themselves. Investment in these sectors is emphasized as a means to higher productivity of the labor force and is justified on the basis of either financial rate of return (as in the case of education) or estimates emerging from production functions (as in the case of Health).

An important implication of the human development approach is that it limits the role of public intervention. Individuals are expected to undertake investment in education, health and nutrition on their pursuit of self reliance. It does not pay any attention to the attitudinal and institutional characteristics that are so necessary for translating individuals levels skills into enhanced productivity at the level of the Economy. These characteristics that, termed as social capital, have been observed to be important determinant of economic growth in south Asian countries.

Human Development Approach

The alternative approach to social sector is that of human development. The term has been defined by the UNDP as 'the process of enlarging people's choices .The concept encompasses empowerment, cooperation, equity in basic capabilities and opportunities, sustainability and security. In this approach people occupy centre stage, and measures such as education, health and nutrition are emphasized from their intrinsic value and not for their role in enhancing their basic capabilities of people.

The emergence of concept of Human development can be traced to efforts by economists such as Amartya Sen who define standard of Living in terms of functioning and capabilities rather than in terms of commodity possession. This approach, which treats human beings as ends in themselves, has strong overtones of neo-Kantian Philosophy. The basic proposition of Kant was that 'all rational beings come under the law that each of them must treat itself and all others never merely as means, but in every case at the same time as end in themselves. To those who adhere to this viewpoint, the human resource approach that treats human capital, which in turn contributes to great human prosperity, is offensive Streeten (1994), following the sane approach terms as humanitarians all those who perceive human beings as ends in themselves as opposed to the human resources developers who emphasize the means or the productivity aspects of human beings. Despite having many distinctions between the two concepts, the two concepts are linked together by the fact that human resource development provides the precondition for human resource development which in turn contributes to economic growth.

Having considered the alternative approaches to social sectors, it is equally important to define social sector and social development. First, social sectors may be defined as those providing social security wherein the term social security is used in the broader connotation. Besides the obvious advantage of linking the concepts of social security and human development, this wider approach provides a comprehensive framework within which social sectors can be analytically tackled. It has been argued earlier that the definition of social sectors cannot be divorced from the purpose for which such a definition is used. If the aim of human development is to provide the basic requirements for the survival and enhance the capabilities of the bottom 20 percent of the population, the two routes to capability enhancement, viz, income generation through direct rural development and employment programme and public provision of education, health and nutrition cannot be considered to be mutually exclusive. In this study, the term social sector includes, among other things, (a) Education, sports Art and Culture, (b) Health and Family Welfare, (c) Water Supply Sanitation, housing and Urban Development (d) Social Welfare And Nutrition (e) Welfare of SC ST (f) Labour Welfare. Often the term social security is linked to the rights of citizens in a country. In this sense, the provision of minimum level of income, education, health and nutrition may be considered to be basic rights of individuals in a society.

Here, it is equally important to define the term social development. According to P.D Kulkarni, "Social Development is a process of transformation in values, institutions and practices, brought about the deliberate use of instruments of policy and planning with the active involvement of concerned people for the purpose of raising their levels of living and quality of life. Social Development refers to the overall progression of the society. However, such modifications in the social order are not possible unless the needs of the people are satisfied. Whereas Economic Development refers to increase in per capita income, per capita value added etc; social development connotes the development of people, quality of life, social welfare etc. The two may be interrelated; and the disparities in one may cause disparities in the other. the nature of relationship between economic and social development, is however, an empirical phenomenon and its explanation lies in the criteria of resource allocation for resource generation and criteria of redistribution of the increased resources for various dimensions of economic and social development. This means that social development and the inequalities in it are at least partly determined by the criteria of resource allocation for the development of human and physical resources and for requisite infrastructure at various levels. These are crucial interdependent factors of economic and social development, but the extent of simultaneity and proportion of development of these factors certainly affect social development and the disparities therein. Thus, we presume that the criteria of resource allocation can explain social development and the forms of disparities in it.

In this context, it is quite relevant to look into linkages that exist between economic development and social development, economic growth and human development and education and human development.

Economic Development and Social Development

Economists have long viewed social development as a byproduct of economic development. Rather social development is often seen as competing with economic development for resource allocation. This is manifested in debates on priority to industrialization or education, or for that matter to a factory or a school. Economists have recently shown a greater awareness of social parameters but their analysis of social development remains loaded input-output considerations.

Many scholars stress the essential unity of the development process and reject any distinction between its economic and social dimensions. They opine that the two are so much blended with each other that it would be unrealistic to treat them separately. Such a position, however, does not leave any scope for structural analysis for development process. In any empirical context, the economic and social aspects of any human situation are generally distinguished from each other. This is reflected in debates on fixing the priority amongst economic or social goals of any development strategy. A distinction between two is justified.

As such, social development is essentially one of the vital dimensions of the overall development process. It denotes the quality of social system in terms of social justice it delivers, social cohesion it maintains, and quality of life it provides for as integral components of regional system. It promises a higher order of living in a dynamic sense. In absence of direct data on various aspects of social development, it is often inferred from a variety of surrogate indicators. These include education, health, nutrition, transport and population indicators.

Human Development and Economic Growth

The linkages that exist between economic growth and human development can be identified. Concepts of Human development and economic growth are not contradictory, rather they are complementary nature. It is essential to overcome the misconception as is harbored by the critics of Human development that stress on human development may be at the cost of the economic growth. At the same time, it is also crucial to focuses attention on the fact that too much of emphasis on either economic growth or on human development may result in unbalanced growth of the economy, which may jeopardize the very process of long-term development. High Gap, has often failed to transform into better living conditions of the masses, particularly where the fruits of development and distribution of income have been uneven. Absence of such coordinated policy measures, which ensures uneven distribution of income and may fail to establish a relationship between economic growth and human development.

In the RBI Study of budgets 2006-07,it is noted that Economic growth can have a positive impact on human development through three different channels: (i) through an increase in the general level of per capita income; (ii) through poverty reduction; and (iii) through higher public expenditure on education, health and related sectors. It is expected that an increase in the general level of per capita income is likely to increase the demand for education and health care, and may improve the human development of a country. Secondly, economic growth associated with poverty reduction may enable the poorer sections of the population to enjoy the fruits of growth and thus, may have a better impact on the human development indicators.

In any economy it is the poorer sections of population who are more deprived of human development elements. The third channel through which the growth can improve human development is through the increased public expenditure on social sectors. Economic growth by increasing the revenue base of the economy may enable the State to spend more on the social sectors. Obviously, this is dependent both on the buoyancy of revenue collection resulting in a softening of the Stat budget constraint and on the political willingness to allocate proportionately for the social sectors. Thus, if the economic growth is to have a positive impact on human development, it would be required to have appropriate policies aimed at reducing income inequalities and higher public social sector expenditure and conversely, if the economic growth is to be sustainable in the long run it has to be supported by better human capital (UNDP, 1990).

In an economy, economic growth may be affecting the human development through all the three channels. However, there are studies which have reiterated the importance of public expenditure channel over and above the trickling down channel of economic growth in improving human development.

A cross-country study by looking into the relative importance of growth channel and public expenditure channel in improving life expectancy finds that public expenditure on health care contributed two-third of the improvement in life expectancy and economic growth through poverty reduction contributed only one-third. However, in the case of literacy, the study did not get any concrete evidence in favor of public expenditure on education. Moreover, there are countries like Sri Lanka, which achieved relatively higher human development despite being a developing country. The supported policies followed in Sri Lanka through higher public expenditure on social sectors are widely acknowledged in the literature). An inter-State study on India also reveals that while the disparities in per capita income among the States are increasing, the disparities in social development are coming down, pointing to the importance of public social sector expenditure in achieving human Development.

Education and Economic Growth

T.W Schultzhas given three ratios in relation to education and economic growth

1. Education-labour ratio to show the amount of human effort going into education relative to the total labour force.
2. Education-Income ratio which relates the resources entering into education to consumer income.
3. Education-investment ratio to show the relation between the resources entering into education and the resources going into producible physical capital.

V.N. Kothari mention that Dennison's work about the share of education in the growth rate. Education accelerates human resource development. Education and development are not two different things but two sides of the same coin. P. Naik observed that education lead to development and development should create the motivation for more education as well as provide tools for it. In short, economic growth is necessary but not sufficient for human development.

Public policy concern for human development is always constrained by lack of adequate resources. In financially weak states like ours, the provision for basic choices requires huge investment. Mobilizing resources for human development activities present many challenges and these become compound when on witness the paucity of resources and debt burden in the state.

The issue of positive or negative impact of public debt management in achieving the macro economic objectives has been frequently discussed. Some Economist argue that at best, these programmes do little in the way of improving economic indicators while others have gone so far as to say that programmers worsen the situation.

Emphasis on the growth rate of the macro economic variables has over the years been accepted as the yardstick of progress of a nation. However, it is often overlooked that it is the human being who is the real initiator of growth and development of the economy and therefore deserves to be the main beneficiaries of economic growth.

The state governments incur the bulk of the expenditure on social sectors. Consequently, while the Union Government may be keen on minimizing the social costs of economic reforms, the actual outcome in the sphere depends on the actions taken by the numerous state governments. Indian states differ a great deal from one another in terms of level of levels of social sector attainment as well as the government policies pertaining to them.

In the occasional Papers (RBI), it is noted that, "Investing in people is now well recognized as the prime motive behind various development and poverty alleviation initiatives". At the international level, one sees several initiatives in the 1990s aimed at sustainable economic and social development, which have finally culminated in the shape of the United Nations Millennium Declaration of September 2000, setting out various developmental goals influencing the well-being of people. Education and health sector goals have been recognized as crucial components of the Millennium Development goals. International community is associated with the changing perceptions about the desirability of human capital formation not only as a means, but also as an end in itself. The World Development Report 2003 also notes that one of the initiatives to promote sustainable development in a dynamic world is to empower underprivileged sections of population by increasing their access to education and health. In recognition of the fact that economic prosperity, measured in terms of per capita income alone, does not always ensure enrichment in quality of life, the development strategy adopted in the Tenth Plan in India is also built on the need to exploit synergies between economic growth, desirable social attainments and growing opportunities for all. In line with this broad thinking, it is envisaged that the Government's role will clearly have to expand in social sectors.

An important fact that needs to be noted at the very outset is that, in India, Social sectors, particularly education and health, are the subjects under state government purview to a large extent. Therefore the state governments incur the bulk of the expenditure on social sectors. Consequently, while the Union Government may be keen on minimizing the social costs of economic reforms, the actual outcome in the sphere depends on the actions taken by the numerous state governments. In a federal country like India, the achievement of social development goals depends largely on the initiatives and commitment of the states. Many of the social policy areas are the responsibility of states or are under the concurrent list. While the burden on deficit compression of the centre fell on the government investment expenditure, in the states it was the social sector that bore the burnt.

Against this backdrop the backdrop of the increasing importance being attached to human development both at national and international levels on the one hand and challenges faced by the financially weak states for mobilizing resources for human development, a question that is frequently raised in connection with Public debt management is whether the government has been effective in achieving a positive impact on social and human development in the state. Expenditure on human development in India needs to be look into, in addition to education, public health, sanitation and water supply, basic needs and poverty removal programmes as potential to income generation. In this context, it may be noted that public spending in human development activities yield double return when analyzed in terms of poverty reduction.

The central issue of public expenditure is how the national cake is divided, how resources are allocated to different sectors, how investments are balanced between long and short tem goals, and how resources are distributed to increase or decrease the different locations. The sectors or people or regions sharing a larger slice of the national cake are the government's major concern. Size and composition are the two basic dimensions of government expenditure. The size can be seen in relation to the GNP of a country. It represents the capacity of a government to spend, and thereby, involve itself in people's life through provision of various services and goods. The composition, on the other hand, reflects the priorities of a government. If social development were its major concern, this sector will automatically receive higher allocation.

In the spirit of above observations, the present study intends to examine the pattern of government expenditure o social development as varying between states in India at different levels of economic development. The government involvement in day to day life of the people is of higher order in developing countries than the developed ones. Such an assumption is consistent with the people's expectation and their governments, avowed profession in developing countries. Here government is looked to as the main provider of various provider of social service such as education, health, transport, power, water and housing. The concern for social development is greater in backward states than in the developed states. Developed states are oriented more to economic growth because their value system is characteristically materialistic. Less developed states are by comparison, are more prone to welfarenism, and their government are keen to promote social justice even at the cost of economic efficiency. This is possible only under conditions of relatively higher allocations to the social sector. There are different ways of examining the trends in budget expenditures. One way is to look at social sector expenditures as a proportion to total expenditure.

To understand how robust is the performance of Manipur government as to social and human development, we rely on four types of ratio and additionally, following the UNDP (19991), viz., Public expenditure Ratio(PER) is a measure of the total expenditure of the state government as proportion of NSDP,while the Social Allocation Ratio(SAR) conveys to what extent public expenditure is chanalized for the development social sector(education, health, family welfare, sanitation, water supply, housing, labour welfare etc.) the Social Priority Ratio (SPR)/ Human Development is a sub-set of SAR. To be sure, it reflects the funds allocated towards the cause of the most important social services like primary education & health sanitation and water supply. It is worked out by expressing these allocations as % of expenditure on social services as a whole. It is the product of the aforesaid three ratios, which is equal to social priority expenditure as proportion NSDP. The UNDP Report (1991) also suggested certain expenditure norms that were arrived at after examining the experience of a number of countries and observed to be associated with better human development outcomes. It was suggested that that HPR of 5 percent is essential if a country is to do well on the human development front. This may be achieved in an efficient manner keeping 'the PER moderate (around 25 percent), allocate much of this to social sector (more than 40 percent) and focus on social priority areas (giving them more than 50 percent). The trends in three ratios for our study are presented in Table 5.1.

Table 5.1
Select Social Sector Expenditure Ratios

Year	*Public expenditure Ratio (PER)*	*Social Allocation Ratio (SAR)*	*Social Priority Ratio (SPR)*	*Human Expenditure Ratio (HER)*
1979-80	34.3	42	84.06	11.94
1980-81	34.97	42.83	91.6	13.9
1981-82	35.17	38.6	88.5	12.01
1982-83	36.13	38.51	82.93	11.5
1983-84	34.86	40.22	61.29	15.29
1984-85	38.82	36.88	87.22	12.48
1985-86	41.86	40.18	95.46	16
1986-87	46.8	40.18	89.5	16.71
1987-88	39.6	36.13	88.92	11.38
1988-89	46.06	39.54	93.27	16.64
1989-90	47.92	40.89	91.46	17.92
1990-91	46.45	38.38	89.76	16
1991-92	43.01	40.4	90.49	15.65
1992-93	39.58	42.42	91.23	15.31
1993-94	37.88	39.29	91.62	15.31
1994-95	38.92	38.94	92.19	13.97
1995-96	43.81	38.55	91.93	15.52
1996-97	47	38.7	91.31	16.62
1997-98	42.11	38.51	91.19	14.79
1998-99	35.69	38.56	89.93	12.47

Year	*Public expenditure Ratio (PER)*	*Social Allocation Ratio (SAR)*	*Social Priority Ratio (SPR)*	*Human Expenditure Ratio (HER)*
1999-00	45.63	37.53	92.24	15.7
2000-01	39.9	35.44	92.74	13.12
2001-02	44.39	33.65	90.66	13.97
2002-03	45.04	32.61	91.32	13.41
2003-04	41.05	31.83	89.5	11.69
2004-05	30.2	31.69	89.78	8.61

Notes: All expenditure pertains to revenue components only

1. PER=Total rev.exp/NSDP
2. SAR=Social Services rev exp/Total rev exp
3. SPR=Social Priority rev exp/Social services rev exp
4. HER=Social priority rev exp/NSDP

Source: Finance Accounts Government of Manipur Statistical Handbook (various volumes)

The following salient features emerging from data may be highlighted:

1. In 1979-80, the PER in Manipur was 34.3 percent, which was much above the suggested 25 percent norm. The Fiscal stringency experienced during late 1990s meant no further decline in the subsequent years, it rose to even 45.04percent in the year 2002-003, but it came down all time low at 30.20 percent in 2004-05.
2. In terms of allocations to social Services, the SAR in Manipur was higher than 40 percent norm suggested by UNDP, in the year 1979-80 and 1981, but it declined to 38.60 percent in the succeeding two year i.e1981-82 &1982-83.

3. The SPR in the state is more than the 50 percent norm suggested by the UNDP. In the study period; the ratio fluctuated within a narrow range of 82.93 percent & 95.46 percent.

In line with the above discussion it will be quite relevant if we study calculation of such ratios state wise for India. In this connection the following Table 5.2 will be useful to study. It would be noted that the PER for the central government during the same period under consideration has declined from 17.70 to 13.70. Similarly, the PER of states was noted to have come down from 39.67 to 31.92. It shows a declining trend except for some states of Haryana, Himachal Pradesh, Jammu and Kashmir and Sikkim. Table 5.2 which take reference to major 15 states of the country analysis expenditure on social services and rural development. Wide regional variation across the states were noted with respect to PER in India. The studies by Seeta Prabhu and Chatterjee also calculated PER for 15 major states for the period 1974-91. It was noted that to show an increasing trend in this regard, though the PER for the centre was lower than the stipulated model figure. Where the PER was high, it was not necessary that human development will be higher. This suggested the need for restructuring the expenditure pattern to suit the development priorities.

Social Sector Expenditure including expenditure on education and health amenities, i.e. water supply, sanitation, housing and urban development and other social services have bee expressed as ratio of total Public Expenditure.

The SAR (termed as social sector expenditure ratio in NHDR, 2001) was reported to have increased slightly from 32.89 in 1990-91 to 33.07 in 199-99 for the states, and from 6.40 to 8.20 for the centre during the same period. The suggested ratio is above 40 percent; whereas for the

Table 5.2
A Composition of public spending in India-Some critical Ratios for 1990-91 and 1998-99

	PER		*Developmental exp. Ratio*		*Social Sector Exp.Ratio*		*Health Exp.Ratio*		*Amenities Exp.Ratio*		*Other Social Exp. Ratio*
	1990-91	*1998-99*	*1990-91*	*1998-99*	*1990-91*	*1998-99*	*1990-91*	*1998-99*	*1990-91*	*1998-99*	
A.P	19.74	19.23	72.70	66.11	34.44	33.89	5.17	8.45	3.29	5.48	10.56
Arunachal Pradesh	78.30	65.09	75.72	72.98	25.18	26.27	4.51	5.43	5.77	6.42	1.60
Assam	25.42	20.50	64.75	62.39	30.80	39.07	5.04	4.65	4.74	3.30	4.08
Bihar	23.52	18.37	67.13	57.80	32.94	32.82	5.39	481	2.04	2.20	2.53
Goa	31.44	29.63	78.61	55.20	39.12	27.74	8.41	5.11	9.09	6.52	2.59
Gujarat	19.54	18.76	74.36	71.50	31.40	31.20	5.82	5.41	3.74	5.32	5.10
Haryana	17.58	19.65	69.64	63.31	28.68	26.20	4.04	3.84	3.42	4.08	7.37
H.P	39.72	45.01	71.74	68.84	36.09	34.0	7.09	6.38	7.44	8.76	4.63
J.K	55.92	52.65	66.34	61.96	28.91	24.87	4.98	5.16	7.40	6.44	5.36
Karnataka	21.37	16.48	70.98	67.05	31.81	35.41	6.42	6.02	2.33	4.79	6.91
Kerala	23.95	16.86	64.79	62.45	39.91	33.31	6.76	5.47	2.92	3.69	6.69
M.P	19.36	17.60	71.01	64.61	34.03	36.61	5.02	5.80	4.41	4.32	8.20
Maharastra	16.72	12.09	71.78	61.56	30.33	32.81	5.13	4.84	4.25	4.86	4.80
Manipur	55.17	42.84	73.58	63.37	31.82	32.95	4.40	4.67	5.91	4.88	3.83
Meghalya	45.58	33.63	74.70	69.10	34.71	35.19	6.18	7.22	10.43	8.64	2.47
Mizoram	47.26	-	55.80	71.16	23.23	35.50	3.39	4.93	6.87	11.58	3.50

	PER		*Developmental exp. Ratio*		*Social Sector Exp.Ratio*		*Health Exp.Ratio*		*Amenities Exp.Ratio*		*Other Social Exp. Ratio*
	1990-91	*1998-99*	*1990-91*	*1998-99*	*1990-91*	*1998-99*	*1990-91*	*1998-99*	*1990-91*	*1998-99*	
A.P	19.74	19.23	72.70	66.11	34.44	33.89	5.17	8.45	3.29	5.48	10.56
Nagaland	84.30	-	66.60	53.89	28.33	25.30	6.30	5.39	8.97	7.37	2.91
Orissa	27.98	24.12	68.66	59.94	29.48	32.70	5.02	5.58	3.31	3.80	6.01
Punjab	18.00	19.87	69.55	46.64	26.99	25.09	5.05	4.73	1.77	2.14	4.93
Rajasthan	22.83	21.81	64.88	63.83	34.47	39.12	5.76	6.42	6.39	10.18	4.78
Sikkim	78.30	208.40	80.67	28.13	31.49	14.99	5.93	2.83	8.44	3.71	2.32
T.N	21.13	16.98	31.56	61.74	40.14	38.15	9.44	8.32	4.37	2.86	6.79
Tripura	59.43	44.52	72.81	62.50	37.91	35.96	5.91	4.69	4.34	7.09	10.04
U.P	22.05	18.32	67.89	54.96	29.39	29.37	5.52	4.10	2.30	1.87	4.11
W.B	17.32	15.59	67.78	60.61	40.04	33.86	7.67	6.79	5.07	3.66	4.35
All States	39.67	31.92	69.57	61.76	32.89	33.07	5.88	5.78	3.86	4.63	5.79
Central Government	17.70	13.70	48.10	34.90	6.40	8.20	1.50	1.80	0.40	1.00	1.00

Source: NHDR,2001,p,289-90;Income-poverty and Beyond, Raja. J. Cheliah and Sunrshan p 158-159;NHDR-2001 p,289&290

Notes: PER is the total PER as proportion of GSDP.

Total devt. Exp. includes social services and economic services. Social Sector Exp. including exp.on edu. Health.amenities.i.e. water supply,sanitation,housing and urban development and other social services have bee expressed as ratio of total Pub.Exp.

centre the increase is much below the suggested norm, for states there is need to recast priorities within and in between activities of social sector for achieving the desired results. Wide variations in this regard were also observed (Table 5.2).The study by Seeta Prabhu and Chatterjee in this regard showed a mixed trend. While in case of Hariyana, Tamil Nadu .West Bengal and U. P,the SAR witnessed a general improvement; Kerela Punjab and Gujarat experienced a decline in it over the years. What emerges unambiguously from the foregoing discussion is the state government can restructure its present expenditure pattern in the medium term for promoting human development. The possible avenues for restructuring are briefly discussed below.

If the public expenditure is already high but social allocation ratio is low, the financing of expenditure needs budgetary reassessment to see which area of expenditure can be reduced. If PER and SAR are comparatively high but the ultimate human development is low, the social priority must be increased.

If the problem is low public expenditure ratio (P.E.R), raising this would call for raising revenue and this should be an essential part of the financing strategy Empirically it is observed that the ratio of public expenditure tend to rise with per capita income. However, there are no clear cut rules guiding the appropriate levels of public expenditures relative to GNP or its desirable allocations across sectors at different stages of development.

CHAPTER 6

FINANCE COMMISSION AND STATE'S DEBT

It has been observed in the previous chapters that, in federal fiscal systems, on ground both of equity and efficiency, resources are generally assigned more to the central government, whereas states together with the local government have larger responsibilities. The resultant vertical imbalances require transfer of resources from the centre to the states. States also have different capacities and needs, and this lends to a horizontal dimension to the issue of resource sharing. Neither vertical nor horizontal imbalance is expected to be static. Some of the core provisions regarding sharing of resources are built into the constitution itself. But changes in the economic and fiscal situation warrant a review of the arrangement fro time to time. The constitution has provided for both continuity and change. The finance commission is entrusted with the periodically examining the issues according to the constitutional provisions and the term of reference. In this chapter, an attempt will be made to review of the approach adopted by the Finance Commissions to analyze and minimize the problem of growing indebtedness of the states to the Union government, and in-depth study will be made on the recommendations of three immediately preceding commissions. Central loans to the states have been increasing with varying interest rates and maturing periods. It has introduced complications into the centre-state financial relations.

This dangerous trend drew the attention of the central government and therefore finance commissions have been asked for finding solutions. The problem was referred, for the first time to the second finance commission. But, in spite of the various suggestions of the second finance commission, the fundamental problem of increasing states debt and debt servicing could not be solved. The burden of debt servicing charges continued to increase. Thereafter, a review of the state debt has been the term of reference form the sixth finance commission onwards. Till the Eighth finance commission, the term of reference of the finance commission required them to make an estimation of the non plan capital gap of the states and to undertake a review of the debt position with particular reference to the central loans to the states these commissions were asked to suggest debt relief measures having regard to the overall non-plan capital gap and the purpose for which loans had been utilized and the requirement of the centre. From the ninth finance commission onwards, finance commissions were mandated to review the debt position as a whole and suggest corrective measures in particular references to financial and managerial efficiency. 'The ninth Finance Commission noted with the state of indebtedness of the states which appear to be sliding into vicious cycle. Loans are advanced to specific period and rate of interest. Finance commissions subsequently recommend corrective measures, often across the board, consisting of write offs, extension of maturity periods, and lowering of interest rates, thus converting loans effectively into grants, partially or fully. Periodically repeated debt relief exercises may induce states to overstate their demand for borrowed funds.

Corrective measures should therefore, be formulated in a manner as would provide an in-built incentive for prudent use of borrowed funds. While the tenth finance commission had the mandate to suggest corrective measures keeping in view the financial requirement of the centre, the Eleventh finance commission was required to make an assessment of the debt position off the states as on March 31, 1999 and suggest corrective measures as were deemed necessary, keeping in view the long term sustainability for both the centre and the states. It was for the first time that the phrase 'long term sustainability of debt' was included in the terms of reference to a finance commission. The EFC looked at the relative position of the states in terms of interest payments to revenue receipt which include the states' share of central taxes and grants. The EFC felt that the scheme of general debt relief link to fiscal performance formulated by the TFC needed to strengthen for, the EFC was discontinuing the other scheme of the debt relief recommended by the TFC consider the long tem sustainability of debt for both centre and states. The twelfth Finance commission (TFC) has to contend with difficult fiscal environment in formulating its recommendations. It has to deal with challenges arising from the economic and political environment.

The seventh finance commission (1978) had recommended that small savings loans outstanding against each state at the end of 1978-79 could be consolidated into one loan and treated as a loan in perpetuity. This recommendations however was not accepted by the government of India although it did not concede that the states would not be required to make any repayment during 1978-79. Apart from waiving repayment for 1984-

85, the eighth finance commission did not recommend any further relief or change in the arrangement with respect to the small saving loans. The ninth finance commissions did not recommend any change in the terms and conditions relating to these loans. After examining the matter afresh, the tenth finance commission found that the net amounts available under small savings scheme had been falling in the recent years. From a peak of 50 percent, net collections as a percentage of gross collections had fallen to about 25 percent. The amounts retained by the centre net of interest payment and administrative changes indicated that this source contributed only marginally to its funds. The Tenth Finance Commission noted that small savings schemes had to be run jointly by the centre and the states in order that he benefits of economies of scale reaped, that all states were able to participate and that investors feel protected. It followed that the liability of repayment ought to be shared. Further, if the small savings loans were to be treated as loans in perpetuity, it would mean a rising interest on states in perpetuity. For all these reasons the commission did not favor these loans being treated as loans in perpetuity.

The tenth finance commission rightly noted that the disturbing features of the debt profile of states and its management appear to be the following:

1. Diversion of borrowed funds for meeting revenue expenditure;
2. Use of loans in unproductive enterprises, or enterprises which are potentially productive but are beset by poor performance, and currently yielding low or even negative returns;
3. Non-provision for depreciation or amortization funds in respect of government owned assets, leading to repayment of fresh borrowing.

It should be noted that a bulk of the transfers made by the finance commissions or over 90 percent are unconditional. And there is nothing to state that finance commissions should not give additional or specific purpose transfers. The constitution position is that, "all plan expenditures, special purpose grants and grants etc would come within the scope of Article 275(1) itself". As regards the FRAs, the states are required to take advantage of the benefit of debt restructuring. Similarly, the debt write-off is conditional on reducing revenue deficits. If a state thinks that these are stringent conditions, it can forego these benefits which in any case are not very large.

Surely states have the right to determine their expenditures levels by revenue from own sources. They can also determine the level of capital expenditures by creating surplus in the revenue account. But when the states want spend on wages and salaries not by raising revenues from own sources but by borrowing, the national taxpayer is asked to pay for this service. Similarly, macroeconomic considerations require control over the borrowing of the states.

The constitutions makers are aware of this fact and therefore, stipulated in article 293, when a state is indebted to the central government, it has to obtain the latter's permission to undertake additional borrowing. But in practice there are several ways in which states could have recourse to additional borrowed resources. These include small savings, ways and means advances from the reserve bank of India, public sector enterprises.

Successive Finance commissions have been recommending debt relief to the states by way of rescheduling and some write off in response to the complaints from the states that their repayment obligations to the centre are absorbing a very large part of fresh loans. Prior to the ninth finance commission, the states are allowed the full benefit of loans for externally funded projects like assistance from bilateral aid agencies or international agencies like World Bank, the states' share being restricted to only 70 percent of the aid amount. The states were made eligible for receiving 100 percent of such assistance thanks to the recommendations of ninth Finance commission.

Besides, loans from the centre and market borrowings, the other sources of growth in liabilities in recent years have been loans from financial institutions and the public account liabilities. According to an analysis by the RBI, the overall impact of the rising debt level has reduced the flexibility of states to release funds for basic infrastructure and the social sector.

Some attention was paid to this issue by the central government while drafting the terms of reference to the Tenth and Eleventh Finance commissions in 1992 and 1998 respectively. Both the commissions formulated certain schemes for debt relief to the indebted states which however, were not sufficient to deal with magnitude of the problem. It is necessary that the issue be addressed more seriously while drafting the terms of reference of Thirteenth Finance Commission.

Debt Relief for State Governments Through Finance Commissions

In successive finance commissions, the issue of giving debt relief to the states has been considered, and has been extended by the following ways: (i) consolidation of loans on common terms and with reduction in the interest rates for the future, (ii) revision in the terms of repayment of loans given to states without a lowering of interest rates, (iii) moratorium on interest payments and repayment of principal due in certain years, (iv) write-off of loans or repayments falling due during a specified period, (v) introduction of schemes of debt relief linked to fiscal performance etc. While the Second, Seventh and Eighth Finance Commissions consolidated some of the earlier loans and rescheduled them at lower rates of interest, the Sixth Finance Commission revised the terms of repayment of outstanding loans. The Seventh Finance Commission also recommended that small savings loans outstanding at the end of 1978-79 be converted into loans in perpetuity. This recommendation was, however, not accepted by the central government. Write- off of specific loans also constituted a part of the recommendations of these commissions.

The ninth Finance commission stipulated that repayment on account thereof, already made by the state government by way of principal and interest shall be adjusted against other payments due from the state government. Further, the state plan loans advanced during the five-year period of 1984-89 and outstanding as on 31st March, 1990 were recommended for consolidation and reschedulement for 15 years in the case of all states. During the first five years i.e. 1990-95, repayments were to be less than those due on the then existing basis to the extent of 10 per cent in the case of Andhra Pradesh, Karnataka, Madhya Pradesh, Maharashtra, Orissa, Tamil Nadu, Goa and special category states, 7.5 per cent in the case of Gujarat, Rajasthan and Uttar Pradesh and 5 per cent in the case of Bihar, Haryana, Kerala, Punjab and West Bengal.

The tenth Finance commission took the debt problem of fiscal stress state like Manipur and recommended that a debt relief scheme in two parts, namely, (i) a scheme for general debt relief for all states linked to fiscal performance and (ii) specific relief for states with high fiscal stress, special category states and states with debt problems warranting special attention. This was in addition to a scheme for encouraging retirement of debt from proceeds of disinvestment and equity holding of state governments. The general debt relief scheme of the Tenth Finance Commission measured improvement in fiscal performance by comparing the ratio of revenue receipts (including devolution and grants from the centre) to total revenue expenditure in a given year with the average of the corresponding ratio in the three Immediately preceding years. The performance of each state was measured against its own past performance. Twice the excess of the ratio over the average ratio of fiscal improvement during the preceding three years was recommended for relief on loans contracted during the period 1989-95 and falling due for repayment after 31st March, 1995. The relief was admissible only to the extent of ten per cent of the amount due for repayment from these loans in any year. We observe that the actual relief sanctioned to states based on the Tenth Finance Commission recommendations was Rs.212 crore during the period 1995-2000 compared to the relief of Rs. 565.51 crore (assuming increase in performance by 2.5 percentage points) estimated by the Tenth Finance Commission. A specific relief in the form of write-off of 5 per cent of repayments due in regard to fresh central loans given during 1989-95 and outstanding as on 31.3.95 was also recommended by the Tenth Finance Commission for special category states and three other states (Orissa, Bihar and Uttar Pradesh), considered to have high fiscal stress, as their average ratio of interest payments to revenue expenditure exceeded 17 per cent during 1989-90 to 1993-94. In the case of Punjab, one-third of repayment of principal on special term loans falling due during 1995-2000 was recommended to be waived. However, the quantum of relief is not significant as show in Table 6.1 below. The share of debt relief in the GDP has reduced from 2.95 percent in the sixth finance Commission to 0.17 percent in eleventh, indicating a relative commitment to central debt forgiveness over time. Nevertheless, successive finance commissions have established tradition of unconditional debt forgiveness.

Table 6.1
Debt forgiveness by Finance Commissions

Finance Commissions	*Year of report*	*Debt Relief (Rs. Crore)*
Sixth	1974	197
Seventh	1979	216
Eighth	1984	229
Ninth	1989	98
Tenth	1995	50
Eleventh	2000	340

Source. Economic and Political Weekly, June 26, 2004

Up to the eighth Finance commission, the state wise allocation of relief was linked to the proportion of the indebtedness of the respective states, relative to the size of their economies. However the tenth finance commission introduced the performance liked debt relief scheme, which was continued by Eleventh Finance commission and twelfth Finance commission with certain modifications. The tenth finance commission had recommended a scheme of debt relief for all states liked to fiscal performance. Improvement of fiscal management was measured by comparing the ratio of revenue receipts (including devolution and grants from the centre) to total revenue expenditure in a given year with the average of corresponding ratios in three immediately proceeding years. The performance of each state was measured against its own past performance. Under another scheme proposed by TFC viz. the scheme for encouraging retirement of debt from the proceeds of the disinvestment of equity holdings of state governments not much headway could be made during 1995-00 as only Tamil Nadu could avail of relief of about Rs. 10 crore under this scheme. The EFC discontinued the schemes of debt relief based on disinvestment of fiscal stress and focused only on debt relief linked to improvement in the revenue balance by increasing the extent of potential relief in the fiscal performance liked scheme. The EFC did not consider any special debt relief for the fiscally stressed states, but continued the general debt relief scheme of the Tenth Finance Commission with the following modifications: (i) instead of a factor of 2, a factor of 5 was applied on the ratio of fiscal improvement in terms of revenue receipts to total revenue expenditure (ii) the ceiling of stipulated relief was set at 25 per cent of repayment due in any one year instead of 10 per cent and (iii) in the calculation of revenue receipts, the revenue deficit grants recommended by the EFC under article 275 were to be excluded. This relief was to be available in respect of fresh loans granted during 1995-2000 and outstanding on March, 2000. Although the estimated debt relief was Rs.600 to Rs.700 crore, we have been informed by the Ministry of Finance that till September, 2004, the states qualified for a relief of Rs.131.77 crore only. The states which have benefited under the scheme are Andhra Pradesh (Rs.77.52 crore), Arunachal Pradesh (Rs.1.72 crore), Manipur (Rs.2.47 crore), Tamil Nadu (Rs.7.89 crore) and Punjab (Rs. 42.11 crore). While formulating its views on debt relief the Twelfth Finance Commission took into account the existing levels of state's debt, their fiscal situation and, the TFC recommended debt relief to states in two parts, general debt relief through consolidation of outstanding central loans and debt write off linked to revenue reduction.

General debt relief and debt write off recommended by TFC constitute 9.3 percent and 25.0 percent respectively of outstanding balances of central loans granted up to March 31,2004 and outstanding as on March 31, 2005 for availing the facility of general debt relief, all that states are required to do is o enact fiscal responsibility legislations. Debt relief consists of rescheduled and lowering of interest rate to 7.5 percent. These benefits will be available from the year state enact fiscal responsibility legislations.

General Debt relief: The TFC recommended consolidations of central loans to states contracted till march 31,2004 and outstanding on 31 march 2005 and their reschedulement for afresh term of 20 year at an interest rate of 7.5 percent. The debt swap scheme for states introduced in 2002-03 in substitution high cost central government loans by market borrowing and loans from National saving funds (NSSF). As a result of the debt swap scheme, the amount of outstanding loans from the central government (excluding Delhi) has come down even in absolute terms to Rs.2,30,735 crore at the end of 2002-03 to Rs.205253 at the end of 2004-05. Thus, the debt swap scheme has minimized the benefit of debt consolidation to states. Outstanding debt is the highest for the middle income states, followed by the aggregate benefit as a result of consolidation of loans estimated at rs11, 929crore in terms of deferred repayment over the award period of the TFC. Debt relief as a percentage of total consolidated outstanding debt, special category states, income middle and high-income states, in that order. However, the benefit of consolidation depends on the maturity pattern of outstanding loans by external lending and the share of loans in the centre in the total outstanding debt.

With the TFC recommendations, allowing states to directly access the market for financing the loan component, and allow the states to approach market directly. If, however, some fiscally weak states are unable to rise from the market, the centre would borrow for the purpose of on-lending to such states, but interest rate should be transferred to states on the same terms and conditions as attached to such assistance.

The external assistance pass through states should be managed by a separate fund in the public account fund. All states should set up sinking fund for amortization of all loans including loans from bank, liabilities account of NSSF. The fund should be maintained outside the consolidated fund of the states public account the public account and should not be used for other purpose, except for redemption of loans.

Debt write off: The TFC recommended write off repayment of repayment of central loans from 2005-10, after consolidation and resettlement. The write off is linked to revenue deficit reduction and subject to a state fulfilling a number of conditionalities; under the scheme, the repayments due from 2005-06 to 2009-10 on central loans contracted upto 31.03.2004 and recommended to be consolidated will be eligible for write off. The quantum of write off of repayment will be linked to the absolute amount by which the revenue deficit is reduced in each successive year during our award period. In effect, if the revenue deficit is brought down to zero, the entire repayments during the period will be written-off.

However, the actual write off will be worked out by applying the ratio of repayment due in 2005-10 to the base revenue deficit, with the actual revenue reduction. The scale of debt write off will be generally be lower for fiscally stressed states, because of their higher base year revenue deficit. Therefore fiscally stressed states like Manipur need to effect much higher reduction in their revenue deficits in less fiscally stressed states. The total amount of write off in a year is restricted to the repayments due in that year, after loan consolidation and reschedulement. For a state to become eligible loan write off in a year, cumulative reduction in revenue deficit relative to base year figure should be at least equal or higher than cumulative interest relief obtained by the state as a result of loan consolidation and interest rate reduction. The write off is subject to the further stipulation of a state containing its fiscal deficit at the level of 2004-05. If in any year the fiscal deficit exceeds 2004-05 level, the benefits of write off would not be available, even when all the requirements are met. A zero revenue deficit by 2008-09 will entitle the state to a full write-off all repayments due from 2005-06 on central loans contracted up to march 31, 2004 and consolidated by the TFC.

The condition that reduction in revenue deficit should be at least equal to reduction in interest liability on account of debt reschedulement is inequitable to those states whose interest saving is higher than revenue deficit. These states need to eliminate revenue deficit to be able to derive the benefit of debt relief. In this category fall states like Bihar, Jharkhand Arunachal Pradesh, Meghalya an Tripura and Manipur is under this category. For states like Andhra Pradesh, Chastisgarh and Karnataka interest savings are quite substantial in relation to the base year revenue deficit. Past experience shows that actual performance by states was much below the assessment made by the Finance commissions. Assuming that post-tax devolution non plan revenue deficit states would do all that was expected of them by finance commission, these states would at best succeed in eliminating deficit on their non plan revenue accounts.

These states cannot be expected to eliminate their entire revenue accounts deficits unless the revenue component of their plan is fully met by the plan grants. In this scenario, fiscally stressed states would be denied the benefit of debt write offs. On the whole, the package of general debt relief and debt write-off does not address the problems of severely indebted states like Manipur.

In the case of the few special category states which still have revenue surplus the conditionality to be satisfied is that they should maintain in the base year level of revenue surplus in each year during the award period to benefit the write off scheme. If in any year the revenue surplus is less than that of the base year, they will not get the benefit of a writ off that year. Since almost all the revenue surplus states are highly dependent on the central transfers for their revenues, the maintenance of revenue surplus to enable them to get the benefit of write off will critically depend on such transfers. The benefit of debt write off is not easy to come by. The quantum of debt write off would be linked to the absolute amount by which the revenue deficit.

On the issue of whether the incentive liked to the debt write off scheme will be effective, it depends on how important this relief to each state. Altogether, the write off constitutes just about 43 percent of the total estimated transfer recommended by the 12 finance commission for the five year period and given this a small portion, it is not clear whether the states will respond to the incentive. Of course, an individual state's response to the incentive depends on the magnitude of the adjustment it has take and the volume of gain by responding to the incentive. However, Manipur to get the benefit of debt write off Rs.188.54 crores from 2005-10, the write off as percentage of transfers is 2.74 % only if it is able to eliminate its revenue deficit by 2008-09. Debt servicing of the state in future, thus is likely to become much easier as a large proportion of existing debt burden may be written off.

Single-minded pursuit of fiscal correction to get the benefit of debt relief can have disastrous implications for those states where social and infrastructure investments have been insufficient in the past. Some of the states will have to impose heavy cuts in the development expenditures. Both revenue and capital expenditure need to adhere to the tight schedule to bring down revenue deficits to zero by 2008-09. A more rational approach may be to allow them to have more realistic adjustment path over a longer period. Otherwise they are unlikely to draw the benefits of debt write off on the basis of stipulated yearly reduction in revenue deficits.

Table 6.2
Debt redemption scheme

States (NE)	*Debt relief*		*Repayments Due during 2005-10*	*Annual during Repayments due 2005-10*	*Average revenue Surplus/deficit (2001-02) to 2003-04)*
	Repayment	*Interest*			
Arunachal	19.98	71.73	97.39	19.48	31
Pradesh	507.62	153.87	524.95	104.99	-945
Assam	292.14	27.26	188.54	37.71	-176
Manipur	14.81	56.49	80.27	16.05	54
Maghalya	7.31	50.54	67.85	13.57	-134
Mizoram	21.35	56.06	80.15	16.03	-54
Nagaland	24.76	123.97	117.53	23.51	22
Tripura	887.97	539.92	1156.68	231.34	-1202

Source: Twelfth Finance Commission

A major shortcoming of the debt relief plan of the TFC is that it is confined to only a small part of the outstanding debt of the states viz. loan liabilities to the centre, which constitute only about one sixth of the total's loans which account for 30 percent of the state's borrowing are left out. While lending by the centre has ceased, the states are now required to depend heavily on funds accruing from small savings by borrowing from the NSSF, clearly a cost source. The institutional change envisaged by TFC for state s' borrowing will come to nought unless the states are freed from NSSF and accretions to NSSF are treated as part of the funds in the financial market.

It is necessary to review the planning process and do away with the plan/non-plan dichotomy as the TFC urged. The integrity of the constitutional scheme of transfer s would require all revenue transfers to be mediated by FC. This would imply the plethora of centrally sponsored schemes would end and the plan grants also should come within the purview of the FC with the PC asked to look after only the capital requirement of the state which are deficient in infrastructures.

Regarding the Borrowings by states, the TFC made two important recommendations with regard to the future loan contracting by states. The first one that the centre should restrict its assistance for state plans to only grants and allow freedom to access markets for the loan components of the plan.

In the present dispensation, where plan size determines the borrowings of states, debt has become explosive. Plan size is determined more by development consolidation than by ability of a state to service the debt. The TFC recommended a body like the Australian Loan Council to fix the borrowing limits for states. In Indian, context, constitution of loan council will be a paradigm shift, the way plan size is determined. A Plan size doesn't bear any relationship with the capacity of state to service debts.

The commission has argued that the important institutional changes are required to tackle some of the structural problems in managing government finances. On central change relates to the regime of government borrowing. It has recommended that states, like the centre, must decide their annual borrowing programmer within the framework of their respective fiscal responsibility legislation. In, fact the state government move on a path of fiscal correction, the market borrowing programme of the states will be sustainable and they should not face difficulties in terms of eliciting the necessary prescription. There is also need to let the states access the market directly for their borrowing requirements. Such a practice will bring in the needed fiscal discipline. The overall limit to their annual borrowing from all sources should be supervised by an independent body like loan council. Looking overall, the recommendations of the TFC relating total debt relief to states are far more significant than those made by other previous commissions. The quantum is of relief substantial and the conditional ties are not unreasonable. The critical precondition is passage of fiscal responsibility legislation and the critical fiscal correction expected to be carried out by the states is to bring down the revenue deficits.

From the foregoing discussions, it is clear that the burden of fiscal correction needed by different states vary accordingly. As far as major states are concerned the achievement of milestone laid down but the FRBM Act will depend on their success in improving revenue buoyancy and compressing non-productive revenue expenditures, especially untargeted subsidies. In respect of the smaller states also there is considerable scope for reducing wasteful revenue expenditure, but their revenue will be by and large, be governed by the central transfers which in turn depend on the tax buoyancy of the centre.

The benefits to states arising from consolidation, reschedulement and interest reduction of central Loans as recommended by TFC are considerable. As against the pre-consolidation repayment liability of Rs.44,128 crore, the post-consolidation repayment liability is of the order of Rs.32,200 crore to the states indicating a saving of about Rs.12000 crore. The only pre-condition for receiving the benefits of this scheme is passage of fiscal responsibility legislation. By the time the Finance Commission submitted its report, five states viz. Karnataka, Kerela, Punjab, Tamil Nadu and Uttar Pradesh had passed the legislation.

If the basic policies had been sound such corrective measures and relief suggested by the Finance commissions would have been resorted to equilibrium on the longer term basis. Since the basic manner of extending loans to the states and allocating capital resources was not in consonance with the principles of capital finance, high indebtedness with the attendant high interest liabilities, out of proportion to the basic capacity to service debt would result, particularly because the debt relief schemes can be expected to be replaced. And, as we know, they have become an endemic feature of state finance. Increasing government deficits and a steady accumulated debt have been an adverse impact on the interest rates which caused significant increase in their borrowing costs. Therefore, one solution to the states indebtedness may be giving state government' Financial Autonomy, G Thimmaiah and Hemlata Rao rightly said that the finance commission should recommend to the central Government not to interfere periodically with the financial powers of the state governments. This suggestion may look awkward and embarrassing. But it has got a justification. The finance commission is going to assess the non-plan revenue gap in the current budgets of the state Governments.

While so doing so it has to take into account the revenue potential of the state governments. Many state governments in their scope to raise additional revenue has come down partly because of the in-roads made by central governments into their taxing power and particularly in the field of sale tax. Since the Finance Commission is provided under the constitution to protect the financial interests of the state governments, the finance commission should caution the Central government against tampering with the financial powers of the state Governments. Here it is quite relevant to note the opportunity that the thirteenth finance commissions will have the opportunity to assess the requirements of the states in a holistic manner without making a distinction between the plan and non-plan sides. In particular, it is opportune to take the comprehensive requirements of the social sectors such as basic education and health care to ensure comparable standards of services in these services across the country. The requirement to spend more on public education and healthcare in poorer states is all the more important due to the small presence of the private sector particularly in rural areas in these states.

It will be very difficult to change the share of the states drastically in its recommendations. However, it can make a paradigm shift to change the structure of incentives and accountability as an inherent part of the transfer system. Thus, rather than continuing with the 'gap-filing' approach, the commission can fully equalize expenditures on at least basic healthcare and education. It is possible to design the transfer system to build in incentives even to states that have a better record of providing education and health to improve their services further from quantity to quality. If necessary, the tax devolution percentage can be appropriately adjusted to ensure equalization of social services.

The thirteenth finance commission may also have to think of certain drastic measures in order to arrest the rising levels of debt and debt servicing liabilities of the states. It may be necessary for the commission to estimate the interest liabilities of the states for the year 2011-2016 and arrive at optimum level of interest payments as a percentage of their revenue receipts as well as reduction in revenue deficits. There are at least two measures which could help reduce the burden of the states. First, the thirteenth finance commission, in consultation with the planning commission could recommend that in future the Planning Commission would not give approval for a state plan which is formulated in excess of its estimated resources. As regards market borrowings for financing the plan, the current system needs some modification. The planning commission after a careful assessment of the states' fiscal position could fix an overall ceiling for market borrowings and a sub-ceiling only up to which approval for market borrowings through the Reserve Bank Of India would be given and for the balance amount of states may have to fend for themselves from the market. Keeping in view the high percentage of the revenue components of the states' plans, the finance commission in consultation with the planning commission could recommend that the grant element of the central plan assistance as per financial needs of the backward states.

CHAPTER 7

CONCLUSION, MAJOR FINDINGS AND POLICY RECOMMENDATIONS

Based on the analysis presented in the foregoing chapters, the present chapter aims at highlighting the broad but integrated observations of the study to enable to suggest various policy implications and planning in challenging problems and prospect of public debt management and its impact on human development.

It is evident from the foregoing chapters that central loans constitute an important mechanism for transfer of resources from the centre to the states. Central Loans to states accounts for the largest proportion of the total loans of states (and their total liabilities). Large part of these loans arise in the process of inter Governmental fiscal transfers through the planning commission. These are loans that are combined with grants that are given to state governments to finance state plans. These loans are largely formula based and thus may have very little to do with a states borrowing capability.

The outstanding public debt of Manipur has increased from Rs.29.82 crores in 1972 to Rs.3193.19 crores in 2005. It has increased by more than 107 times. It is also clear that the outstanding central loans to the state have increased to from Rs.28.54 crores in 1972 to Rs.1480.50 crores in 2005. It has increased by more than 51 times. It is also clear from the table that Public debt of Manipur increased from Rs.2982 crores in 1972 to Rs.79.48 crores in 1981. Since then it increased to Rs.236.30 crores in 1988, it has further increased to Rs.3193.19 crores in 2005. Thus, within 17 years, Manipur's public Debt has increased by more than 13 times. Thus, this rapid increase in the Public Debt of the state government shows its ever increasing dependence on loan finance particularly on the central Government. Although the share of central in the state's debt declined in the recent years, it continued to be the largest share in the state's debt and it is found that the magnitude of central loans to the state has enormously increased during the study period. It is clear that income effect of thee financial burden of interest charges on central loans has been fluctuating and in some years, it was below 3 percent and the magnitude of the percentage was also small. This is due to the debt relief given by the Finance Commissions. The interest charges as a proportion of the states revenue expenditure has been fluctuating, it was 4.09 percent in 1980-81 and declined to 1.94 percent in 1983-84. Then it started rising absolutely from 1990 till 2005-06.

The findings regarding, the decision about the burden of public debt is that the burden would be measured only with reference to the growth of national income and that the growing Public debt need not cause any concern so long as National Income rises adequately. This point of view has a special appeal to a special category state like Manipur where Public debt plays a very significant role in mobilizing financial resources for undertaking a higher volume of investment which otherwise would not be possible and in creating a suitable institutional framework for effective implementation of monetary policy. However, it is found out that, the rate of growth of central loans and that of state's net domestic product are almost steady. The rate of growth of outstanding central loans were more than that of that of NSDP in the following years, in 1980-81,82-83,83-84.85-86 to 88,1990-91.1994-95,1998-99.2000-01,2002-03. This is certainly not good.

Coming to the burden of debt-repayment and servicing, it is seen that, it started to increased abruptly from 2000-01 and it had almost the same in the subsequent three years but it fell down to 6.43 percent in 2005-06. This shows that economic development burden has increased year after year. The position is bound to worsen further in the coming years unless some corrective measures are evolved and applied. It is welcome decision of the central Government to include this question in terms of reference of reference to the Twelfth Finance commission which looked into the specific debt problems and corrective measures. This is indicative of the extent of misutilisation of the central loans to the state in the name of capital expenditure. The central loans are not accompanied by the increase in the rate of asset creation. If the borrowed funds are used for asset creating public projects, the income of the state is bound to increase. The cost of the burden would be then off set by the benefits that the debt-creation confers. However, at least the part of the rise in state income may be attributed to the rise in central loans which provided funds for public investment.

In the findings regarding the social and human development impact, what emerges unambiguously is that, the state maintained the share of social services in total revenue expenditure at pre-crisis period levels, which was 42.83 percent, declined to 38.60. If the public expenditure is already high but social allocation ratio is low, the financing of expenditure needs budgetary reassessment to see which area of expenditure can be reduced. If PER and SAR are comparatively high but the ultimate human development is low, the social priority must be increased. If the problem is low public expenditure ratio, raising this would call for raising revenue and this should be an essential part of the financing strategy. Empirically it is observed that the ratio of public expenditure tend to rise with per-capita income. However, there are no clear cut rules guiding the appropriate levels of public expenditures relative to GNP or its desirable allocations across sectors at different stages of development. The recognition of the right to education as a fundamental right, and the consequent responsibility thrust on state government to ensure that universal primary education is achieved in the near future makes it imperative to increase allocations to this sector.

Given the high level of states outstanding liabilities, certain corrective measures are inevitable. Corrective measures leading to sustainability of debt can be effective only when state governments make a persistent attempt to put their finances on sound footing by additional revenue effort, expenditure compression and re-prioritization in line with the restructuring plans. Bailouts through write-offs/ waivers can never be a long term solution. Waivers of loans and interest should be strictly restricted so as to avoid moral hazard problems and encourage debt repayment discipline. Relief of debt should be incentivised by clearly linking it with simple monitor able reforms or processes.

Against this backdrop, any attempt to suggest solutions to the problem of burden of burden of union loans on the states should have both long term and short term perspectives. This is essential because any realistic solution should go to minimize the immediate financial burden of the Union loans on the states, as otherwise they will not help much in solving their immediate financial problem. At the same time, these short term solutions should not become adhoc measures as in the case of the recommendations of the finance commissions which after temporarily easing the financial emergency will perpetuate the basic problem in the long run.

Before proceeding further in detail, we may analyze certain solutions without making any in depth study of the problem. Mr K. Venkataraman has advocated that in future union loans should be related to the nature of the schemes o be undertaken by the state governments. He has suggested that:

1. Union loans for such 'non productive social infrastructure facilities as roads and housing should be provided directly by the Union government at 3% interest rate.
2. Union loans for productive schemes like irrigation, electricity generation, industrial and commercial undertakings should be channeled through a central loan council, consisting of central Loan council, consisting of representatives from the state governments. Reserve Bank of India, Planning Commission and Union Finance ministry, which should function strictly on commercial principles. These loans should bear an interest rate of 6 percent.
3. And the presently outstanding Union Loans should be consolidated and standardized with regard to their interest rates and repayment period.

Proposals made by Mr Venkataraman to distinguish between socially productive, but financially non productive and financially productive proposes of state's borrowings from the Union is realistic. But his suggestion to encourage the states to borrow from the market (which suitably include ways and means, requirements and relief works), is most unrealistic. His short term solution though inconsistent with his long term solutions, has already been implemented by Union government on the recommendation of sixth finance commission. It may be recalled in this context that the sixth Finance Commission was asked to suggest a National Relief Fund for assisting such states which would be affected by natural calamities to which both the union government and the state governments should contribute from their own normal revenues. The sixth Finance commission ruled out the case for such relief fund and instead, suggested that states should prepare special plans for such areas and integrate them into their five year plans.

Another short term solution is rescheduling the existing loans by extending the period of repayment from the existing fifteen years and twenty five years for medium and long term loans respectively to twenty and thirty years respectively. A similar recommendation has already been made by the sixth finance commission and has been accepted by Union government only in the case of some loans. However, our contention is that it should be uniformly and be made applicable to all loans. Third, the rate of interest charged on Union loans for socially productive schemes such health and education should not exceed the cost of borrowing by the Union Government. This may also become a long term policy measures. Finally, the rate of interest charged by reserve bank of India for ways and means advances should not exceed the treasury bill rate.

D.M Nanjundappa has suggested that the future union loans to the states should be linked to the stage of development of each state government. For this purpose, he has classified the schemes of development into three categories: (i) self liquidating, (ii) socially productive and (iii) unproductive. He has recommended that plan assistance for unproductive schemes should be given to all states entirely in the form of grants rather than loans, and the loan content of the plan assistance should vary directly with the stage of development achieved by each state. However, his suggestion refers to future loans; as a result they become long term solution unless they are made to apply to the past loans also. If that is done, most of the loans for unproductive purposes should be written off and other loans will have to be adjusted according to the relative proportion of loan grants contents which is not easy task for the reason mentioned. For an important drawback of this suggestion is that the Union government will have to keep on estimating the relative stage of development of each state for each year or plan period in terms of his suggested development index, which is time consuming and unreliable in view of the all too obvious statistical problems involved in estimating it. The report of the study team on centre state relationships submitted to the administrative Reform commission has analyzed the problem of union loans to the states and has made certain interesting suggestions to solve the whole problems of Union Loans to the states. For this purpose, the study team has classified purpose loans viz. share of small savings and ways and means advances. These are entirely non-plan loans but like market borrowings are available to the states for any purpose. Therefore the study team has recommended that repayment obligations of these loans should remain entirely the responsibility of states. Second, loans utilized by the states for relending to third parties for both plan or non-plan purpose. In this case, the study steam has recommended that a state should be able repay these loans out of the recoveries effected from them and hence these loans need not pose any problem to the states except that their difference to the task of recovery should be dispensed with. Third, loans which are given for specific purposes and utilized by the states towards direct expenditure for plan and non-plan purpose. Most of these loans are utilized for plan and non plan purposes.

The study Team has recommended that these loans in future should never be allowed to be used for revenue expenditure purposes and it has proposed the following schemes for this type of Loans.

1. They should be available only for financially productive schemes though in special cases some financially non-productive but socially productive schemes may also be encouraged with these loans.
2. For the remaining schemes (both economically and socially unproductive schemes), assistance should be given in the form of revenue and capital grants for the respective for the respective unproductive purposes should be tied to each an every schemes so that the states will not be able to divert these earmarked fund for the other purposes.
3. Loans for productive purposes should be non-repayable but should bear in appropriate rate of interest with an option that a state that a state should however be free to refund the whole or part of such loan at anytime. the loan should be tied to a scheme or a group of schemes as may be prescribed and a state should have the option of taking repayable loan on the useful terms if it feels that the terms of a non-repayable loan are less advantageous.

The study team has maintained that its proposal of non repayable loans for productive schemes will be a novel feature. Such loans will finance schemes and hence will be comparable to the investments made by the union government in public sector enterprises. Just as these enterprises are expected to pay dividends on investments, state government should likewise assure the union government of a minimum return by way of interest charges on such non-repayable loans.

The study team has recommended that the planning commission, in consultation with the ministry of finance and other concerned minister, should identify the productive schemes and lay down norms for repayable loans. The rate of return that a scheme should be required to yield may vary from scheme to scheme and there need to be a single minimum rate for all schemes. Finally, the study team has opined that miscellaneous development loans must be dispensed with.

The study team has rightly recognized one important drawback of its recommendation, namely, that the suggested no repayable loan will reduce the flow of funds to the union government which in turn will reduce the flow of funds to the Union government which will in turn reduce financial resources available for assisting the state governments. However, it has maintained that widening gap between fresh loans and loan repayments shows that even if a moratorium were placed on repayment, the Union government will have sizable capital resources left from which to provide financial assistance to the states.

The long-term solutions suggested by the study team are worth serious consideration of the government of India. But these suggestions are not integrated with any short term solutions to ease the immediate financial burden of Union loans on the states.

No federal Government can have a short or long term practical relevance unless it begins with measures to chop the extravagant and populist expenditure of the state. The state should rationalize its expenditure policy. The states expenditure policy is defective insofar as the development the non-development has risen rapidly. The non-developmental revenue expenditure is dominated by the outlays on servicing the state's debt particularly central loans. The non-developmental capital expenditure is dominated by the amortization charges of the state debt. Such tendency should be checked.

The state, on its part, will have to take stricter steps to generate more resources for investment. The state government does not exhibit enough political courage in the levy of new taxes and raising the rates of existing taxes. There is no doubt that the state has not been able to mobilize financial resources commensurate with the rising expenditure, mainly because of the its inability to tax adequately the agriculture sector.

The centre should increase the devolution of taxes, duties and grants to the state. Thus on the one hand, amounts to the recognition of the right of the state on national resources and, on the other hand, reduce their dependence on the centre for resources in the form of loans. Reduced dependence on plan finance means reduced dependence on Central loans. Therefore, a dynamic pattern of fiscal transfers from the centre to the states should be evolved so that not only the gap in the non-plan revenue and capital accounts of the state is fully bridged but also the state is enabled to emerge as a financially viable unit of the Union.

Regarding the Loan policy of the state, the problem can be divided into two categories (1) that which relates to past debts and (2) that which relates to future debts. It is suggested that the problems of existing central loans may not be tackled merely through rescheduling of repayment.

The existing loans may be classified in to productive and unproductive ones. The latter should be outright written off and former should be rescheduled and made softer. Within the framework of this policy guidance, the following suggestions are worth considering.

Rescheduling of the terms of the terms of repayment and writing off certain loans made for socially and financially unproductive purposes are short term measures. It is relevant to mention here that there are certain loans given in the past by central government for such purposes as meeting a part of the expenditure of the natural calamities, maintenance of law and order and tackling of insurgency problems.

It may be noted that the major part of the plan assistance is invested in infrastructure projects and in social services like health, education, roads, welfare etc. These investments do not yield direct tangible monetary returns to the state and therefore the plan expenditure on these items should be in shape of grants. It is suggested to write off the interest payments due on such loans and convert the principal amount into grants. The central government should provide grants to the state for such works in future. It will reduce the allocational burden of Union loans on the state. There has to a time lag between plan investments and flow of benefits from such investments. The time lag has to be reflected in terms of repayment. Therfore, in the case of such loans, there should be an initial period of such moratorium both on capital and interest payment and the period should correspond with the expected time taken for the fructification of such schemes. The repayment schedule should with the maturity of such schemes. Besides, these loans may carry rates equivalent to the estimated internal rate on each project.

The states' borrowing powers are restricted unduly by the constitution under Article 293 (1 and 3). The Sarkaria

Commission has taken the view that "it should apply only to long and medium term borrowing fro the open market and not to borrowing from financial institutions or short term for less than one year.

It can be done under Article 293(4) and no amendment of the constitution shall be needed for this. This will give more elbow room to the state. D.M. Nanjundappa has rightly suggested that the future Union Loans to the States should be linked to the stage of development of each state and purpose for which Loan is sought by the State Government. For this purpose, he has classified the schemes of development into three categories, namely (1) self Liquidating, (2) Socially productive and (3) unproductive. He has recommended that the Plan assistance for unproductive schemes rather than Loans, and the Loan content for the schemes s of socially unproductive nature less than the productive nature, and besides, the loan content assistance should vary directly with the stage of development achieved by each state. However, his suggestion refers to future loans and as a result they become long term solutions unless they are made to apply to the past loans also. If that is done, then most of the loans for unproductive purposes should be written off and other loans have to be adjusted according to the relative proportion of loan grant contents which is not an easy task for the reason mention below. For, an important drawback of this suggestion is that the Union government will have to keep on estimating the relative stage of development of each state foe each year or plan period in terms of his suggested development index, which is time consuming and unreliable in view of the all too obvious statistical problems involved in estimating it. Besides it creates uncertainty in regard to the quantum of grants and loans to which state becomes entitled in each year/plan period. This means the state governments cannot reliably estimate in advance their share in the plan assistance from the Union government under each five year plan.

What emerges from the above study boils down to what Prof. Thimmaih writes- "The only solution to this problem is to reduce the size of the loan assistance to the states". If the central government is interested in assisting the states in development activity, as far as possible, all non-self liquidating projects should be assisted by grants. The loan assistance should be categorically confined to self-liquidating (revenue yielding) projects. This should exclude irrigation projects which are presently classified as self-liquidating.

The writings of the Fourth Finance Commission are still resounding in our ears that the entire question of indebtedness of states should be reviewed 'as much in the interest of the states as that of the government of India and that 'in the interest of financial soundness, such an enquiry ought not be delayed any further. The Thirteenth Finance Commission, no doubt, will have to perform a right rope walk. It may be repeated once more that the vice like debt trap is fast closing in on the state and unless multipronged strategy is not adopted to stem it, the state is likely to reach the point of debt trap. Another major issue, which has not received much attention, is the maturity pattern of market loans vis-à-vis central government loans. The central government loans to states are given for a period of 25 years with a moratorium of five years. In contrast, market loans normally have a maturity period of 10 years with bullet repayment at the end of the maturity period.

Regarding debt service burden, the level of borrowing has to be maintained at a sustainable level and resource requirements may be financed more through increasing revenue receipts and economy in development expenditure, which cuts into resources required for sustaining social and economic infrastructure.

Expenditure on the police also needs to be reduced through better public co-operation in maintaining law and order and mobilizing social defense through voluntary service from the public. With the massive growth in unemployment in Manipur, there is likely to be corresponding growth in crimes originating from unemployment and poverty, leading to higher expenditure on police and law and order

Here, it will be useful to highlight some recommendations made by Rajendra R. Vaidya and other related observations to enable to suggest various feasible policy implications.

1. There is a need to re-examine at entire federal fiscal transfer mechanism. If this transfer mechanism is unable to deal both the vertical and horizontal gaps then state governments would be forced to depend increasingly on debt to finance expenditures.
2. The entire system of fiscal transfers needs to be made more transparent and predictable so that the uncertainty about the exact amount of resources a state would have at its disposal in the future can be substantially reduced. One possible of way of achieving this would be to do away with the distinction between plan and non plan assistance to states.
3. Loans from the national government are subject to an "ex post efficiency risk". It arises because of a lack of incentive for the sub national government to exert adequate effort while under taking the project financed by the loan. This lack of incentive in turn arises because of the inability of the national government to make a credible threat of not refinancing debt.

The threat of non-refinancing can be made credible in a system where national government only makes capital grant allocations (through a system which uses transparent economic allocation criteria and has in place a good monitoring system). The 12th finance commissions recommendation that the center transfer funds to states only in terms of tax shares and grants alone and not through loans should be vied in this light.

4. The financial markets in India are not in position to discipline state government borrowing. The following measures need to be taken if markets can depended to enforce disciple on states.
5. Abolish SLR.
6. Improve accounting standards and bring uniformity in the way state governments present their budgets.
7. Have a mechanism in place such that policy responds to market signals.
8. Evolve a clear procedure of rescheduling debt in case a state government either defaults or is close to defaulting its interest and debt repayment obligations.
9. In the medium term, while the institutions needed for market discipline are being built, a rule-based control on state government borrowing seems to be a workable option. Rules that would prohibit states from raising loans to fund current expenditures and a maximum specified debt service to revenue ratio look particularly attractive.
10. Currently, it is too early to pass judgment on the success or failure of the FRLs but given the inadequacies of the over all inter governmental

fiscal transfer mechanism and the fact that not all states have enacted such a legislation its immediate influence on the states' debt position is likely to be negligible. Further more with the central government itself putting its own FRL on "pause" the states have little incentive to be serious about their own FRLs. In the longer term though with proper institution building the FRLs are may possibly be successful.

11. There is an urgent need to force state governments to abandon the current provident fund scheme for state government employees that creates an un-funded debt and move to a fully funded scheme.
12. The states governments should consider the creation of a trust fund that would manage contingent liabilities especially loan guarantees. Unless this is done state budgets would always be at risk from unforeseen events like defaults on debts guaranteed by it.

In this context, it is quite relevant to analyze a study of debt sustainability at state level (RBI) by Indira Rajaraman and others, the study observed that Fiscal responsibility legislation enacted by states can be strengthened by enacting a formal ceiling on incremental borrowing by law. The limit on market borrowings of the state government each year is fixed by the ministry of finance in consultation with the Planning Commission. As already mentioned, the borrowing limit extends only to market borrowings and borrowing from the Centre as a part of institutional lenders like LIC and GIC. Although the total quantum of this borrowing is in principle limited by the size of Plan expenditure agreed to by the Planning Commission, a systematic procedure for ensuring that the limits are adhered to has been introduced only very recently. The Loan Council recomended by the

TFC, if operationalised, will provide a more effective cap, but one that may be at odds with the fiscal deficit correction path in the states' individual FRBM legislation. Finally, the limit does not encompass borrowing from the National Small Saving.

Funds (NSSF) against small savings collections in the state, and states' own small savings deposit collection schemes. States influence the collection under the small savings through aggressive marketing of small saving schemes. In order to impose a hard budget constraint on the states, the overall borrowings including borrowing from all sources should be capped. Where there is unforeseen variation in autonomous borrowings such as small savings flows, corresponding adjustments need to be made under discretionary borrowings. The only other option to a formal state-specific ceiling covering global borrowing from all sources, is to let plan assistance. States are also free to take what are called negotiated loans from the market determine risk premia on state debt. In the Indian context, however, this will lead to fiscal collapse in the highly indebted states. A formal ceiling may in effect be the only way by which to restore sustainability in these states.

The Twelfth Finance Commission, in consultation with the planning commission would recommend that in future planning commission would not give approval for a state Plan in excess of its estimated resources. As regards market borrowing for financing the Plan, the current system needs some modification

The twelfth finance commission recommended a body like the Australian Loan council (ALC) to fix the borrowing limits for states. The government of India accepted this recommendation and indicated that this would be implemented in a phased manner. There is no indication about the role of the planning commission in the changed scenario It seems that planning Commission's role would be restricted to determining plan grants to states, while the propose Loan council would determine loan component of state plans. While better off states would able be able to access to the market at reasonable terms, backward states would be wore off. They may have to pay a premium over that paid by other states as their credit worthiness would be lower and risk perception higher among lending agencies. Weakness in the finances of some state governments manifested in the widening of the spread and under subscription of their market borrowing in 2004-05.

The Planning Commission, after a careful assessment of the state's fiscal position would fix an overall ceiling only u[to which approval for market borrowing through the RBI of India would be given and for the balance amount the states may have to find for themselves from the market.

Central transfer with regard to the reduction in the interest burden, an important area which needs to be addressed is the interest rate on funds for centrally sponsored schemes (CSS) and those for externally aided projects (EAP). Significantly, these two together account for a sizeable proportion of total fresh loans and advances from the central government. It could be noted that the interest cost on central loans at present exceeds 10 percent. Aligning the interest rate on these funds with the actual cost (of central government could make a major dent in the interest burden of the states. Similarly, states also need to focus on the interest rate offered by them on their public account borrowings, which are far above market interest rates. Regarding the interest rates on small savings schemes, it is quite relevant to mention what the Reddy Committee's recommendation that interest rates on small savings schemes should be benchmarked to the secondary market yields of the government securities market. Accordingly, the central government, since 2000-03 is aligning the interest rates on various saving schemes). States could align interest rates on their small savings schemes to market rates. States, apart from small savings and PF collections, also holds deposits (in some cases with chequeable facility) under public accounts. Thus functioning identically like a bank without safeguards of prudential regulations or provisioning requirements.

In India, transfer from the centre to states constitutes a large proportion of Planning commission transfers. Linkages between loan disbursement from the planning commission for capital projects and actual spending on capital project is weak. It is necessary to review the planning process and do away with the plan/non-plan dichotomy as the TFC urged. The integrity of the constitutional scheme of transfer would require all revenue transfers to be mediated by FC. This would imply the plethora of centrally sponsored schemes would end and the plan grants also should come within the purview of the FC with the PC asked to look after only the capital requirement of the state which are deficient in infrastructures.

There is an urgent need to change the modality and mechanics of planning since the main culprit of the fiscal crisis in the states is the plan. The principal difficulty arises because plan size (which determines the size of loans from center) has never been linked to sustainable levels of state debt. No state government can or does refuse to take these loans because it does not see itself in a position to repay the loans nor does the central government refuse to give loans to state governments like Manipur whose financial position is weak. Legally the states are under no obligation to ask for or accept loans from the Union Government. Thus, it can be observed that, the mounting burden of central loans on state's finances as well as unauthorized overdrafts of the state governments are the prominent factors which have affected the gamut of Central-state financial relations in the recent past. The problem is that in the past fiscal reform period, the approach to financing the state plans hasn't undergone a change. All of it continues to be what it was earlier, even though the entire fiscal regime has undergone fundamental changes. The result is that it is impossible for the states to finance their plans in a manner that doesn't add to their fiscal woes.

The resource position of the states is so poor that they cannot even finance the same plan size as last year. Yet they are committed to a plan size that cannot be lower than last year given that they have to meet the tenth five year targets in terms of investment. And this is to the fact that no state government/political party wants a smaller plan; a bigger plan even if partially unfunded is preferred to a fully funded smaller plan.

Another finding of the study is the worrisome aspect of state debt management revealed in this exercise is the changing maturity structure of states' debt towards shorter dated securities in recent years. This trend is prominent in fiscally weak states. To, conclude, the debt management policy should ensure that in a deregulated financial regime, the states are able to borrow at terms comparable to that of central government so that the spread of interest rates between the centre and state declines. The higher premium on state government debt vis-a-vis the centre goes against the fundamental objectives of debt management, which aims at minimizing the cost of debt servicing by eliminating market fragmentation. In this context, the Twelfth Finance Commission's recommendation that "The central government should not act as an intermediary for future lending and allow states to approach market directly" hopefully would achieve the parity in interest rates but its success would critically depend on the improvement in the overall fiscal health of the individual states.

Coming to the Debt relief, on the whole, the package of general debt relief and debt write-off does not address the problems of severely indebted states like Manipur. Single-minded pursuit of fiscal correction to get the benefit of debt relief can have disastrous implications for those states where social and infrastructure investments have been insufficient in the past.

A major shortcoming of the debt relief plan of the TFC is that it is confined to only a small part of the outstanding debt of the states viz. loan liabilities to the centre, which constitute only about one sixth of the total. NSSF loans which account for 30 percent of th state's borrowing are left out. While lending by the centre has ceased, the states are now required to depend heavily on funds accruing from small savings by borrowing from the NSSF, clearly a cost source. The institutional change envisaged by TFC for state's borrowing will naught unless the states are freed from NSSF and accretions to NSSF are treated as part of the funds in the financial market.

The most important reform of the borrowing regime would be to introduce an aggregate borrowing cap and allow for greater flexibility over the choice of borrowing instruments within the cap.

The problem of excessive inherited debt of poor states certainly needs to be addressed; provision of conditional debt relief may not be the best way forward.

The foregoing analysis shows that mere rescheduling of

repayment does not provide a rational and realistic solution to the problem of the Center's loans have to be reclassified according to the critter suggested by us and thereby determine de nova the indebtedness of the states and the reschedule the repayment considering the life of the remunerative asset and the intensity of payoff. Here, it is quite relevant to quote what D.M Nanjundappa noted, "While the actual proportion of grants and loans for any spectrum can further be argued and adjusted, the principle of varying proportions favoring relatively poorer states and reflecting the repaying capacity of investment seems absolutely essential in any realistic solution to the problem of the center's loans to the states".

In the interest of achieving balance in loan assistance, the poorer states should not be strained with increased debt servicing liabilities On the contrary, in the process of rationalizing and enabling sound debt management of the states, the total size of the debt of poorer states should be prevented from undue rise by transferring more resources to them by way of grants until they become viable to manage higher debt burden.

Major Findings

A review of various aspects of problems and prospects of public debt management and its impact on social and human development brought to the fore several interesting insights. The main findings emerging from our study now may be summed up as follows:

1. It is evident from the foregoing chapters that central loans constitute an important mechanism for transfer of resources from the centre to the states. Central loans to states accounts for the largest proportion of the total loans of states (and their total liabilities).

Large part of these loans arise in the process of inter Governmental fiscal transfers through the planning commission.

2. The findings regarding, the decision about the burden of public debt is that the burden would be measured only with reference to the growth of NSDP and that the growing Public debt need not cause any concern so long as NSDP rises adequately. This point of view has a special appeal to a special category state like Manipur where Public debt plays a very significant role in mobilizing financial resources for undertaking a higher volume of investment which otherwise would not possible and in fostering the growth of capital and money markets and in creating a suitable institutional framework for effective implementation of monetary policy. However, it is found out that, the rate of growth of central loans and that of state's net domestic product are almost steady.
3. Coming to the burden of debt-repayment and servicing, it is seen that, it started to increased abruptly from 2000-01 and it had almost the same in the subsequent three years but it fell down to 6.43 percent in 2005-06. This shows that economic development burden has increased year after year. The position is bound to worsen further in the coming years unless some corrective measures are evolved and applied.
4. The government of Manipur has been often resorting to ways and means advances and overdrafts from the centre, although in recent years, no. of days and occasions of state's overdraft reduced.
5. Manipur government's activities are not restricted as only to development activities and to maintain law and

order which has necessitated use of borrowed funds for unproductive purposes such as modernization of police force, security to government officials, etc. The centre should bear all the expenses incurred in maintaining law and order, on the other hand expenditure on the police needs to be reduced better public cooperation in maintaining law and order and mobilizing through social defense through voluntary Service from the public.

6. It may be noted that the major part of the plan assistance is invested in infrastructure projects and in social services like health, education, roads, welfare etc. These investments do not yield direct tangible monetary returns to the state and therefore the plan expenditure on these items should be in shape of grants.
7. The mismanagement of debt is another reason for the present state's debt problem. In theory debt can be justified and welcomed on the grounds that it should be directed towards predictive investments which yield net profits. But, this not the case in the special category state like Manipur which needs huge investments in social infrastructure, as investments in these areas yield no profit; aggravates the debt servicing burden.
8. The findings regarding the social and human development impact, what emerges unambiguously is that, the state maintained the share of social services in total revenue expenditure at pre-crisis period levels, which was 42.83 percent, declined to 38.60.
9. In the interest of achieving balance in loan assistance, the poorer states should not be strained with

increased debt servicing liabilities On the contrary, in the process of rationalizing and enabling sound debt management of the states, the total size of the debt of poorer states should be prevented from undue rise by transferring more resources to them by way of grants until they become viable to manage higher debt burden.

Policy Recommendations

Based on the analysis made above, the following policy intervention deserves necessary attention for adoption:

1. The only solution to this debt problem is to reduce the size of the loan assistance to the states. If the central government is interested in assisting the states in development activity, as far as possible, all non-self liquidating projects should be assisted by grants. The loan assistance should be categorically confined to self-liquidating (revenue yielding) projects. This should exclude irrigation projects which are presently classified as self-liquidating.
2. Manipur government's activities are not restricted as only to development activities and to maintain law and order which has necessitated use of borrowed funds for unproductive purposes such as modernization of police force, security to government officials, etc. The centre should bear all the expenses incurred in maintaining law and order, on the other hand expenditure on the police needs to be reduced better public cooperation in maintaining law and order and mobilizing through social defense through voluntary Service from the public.

3. It may be noted that the major part of the plan assistance is invested in infrastructure projects and in social services like health, education, roads, welfare etc. These investments do not yield direct tangible monetary returns to the state and therefore the plan expenditure on these items should be in shape of grants. It is suggested to write off the interest payments due on such loans and convert the principal amount into grants. The central government should provide grants to the state for such works in future. It will reduce the allocational burden of Union loans on the state. There has to a time lag between plan investments and flow of benefits from such investments. The time lag has to be reflected in terms of repayment. Therfore, in the case of such loans, there should be an initial period of such moratorium both on capital and interest payment and the period should correspond with the expected time taken for the fruitification of such schemes. The repayment schedule should with the maturity of such schemes. Besides these loans may carry rates equivalent to the estimated internal rate on each project. The state Government should urge the central government and finance commission to write off loans invested in infrastructure projects and in social services.
4. State Government needs to ascertain the current and long term financial needs of the state and to maintain strict financial discipline. This is possible, firstly by maximum resources mobilization so that heavy dependence is avoided on the one hand and various programmes for increasing the state's own resources in shortest possible time can be taken.

5. Another short term solution is rescheduling the existing loans by extending the period of repayment from the existing fifteen years and twenty five years for medium and long term loans respectively to twenty and thirty years respectively. A similar recommendation has already been made by the sixth finance commission and has been accepted by Union government only in the case of some loans. However, our contention is that it should be uniformly and be made applicable to all loans. Third, the rate of interest charged on Union loans for socially productive schemes such health and education should not exceed the cost of borrowing by the Union Government. This may also become a long term policy measures. Finally, the rate of interest charged by reserve bank of India for ways and means advances should not exceed the treasury bill rate.
6. Reduced dependence on plan finance means reduced dependence on Central loans. Therefore a dynamic pattern of fiscal transfers from the centre to the states should be evolved so that not only the gap in the non-plan revenue and capital accounts of the state is fully bridged but also the state is enabled to emerge as a financially viable unit of the Union.
7. In the interest of achieving balance in loan assistance, the poorer states should not be strained with increased debt servicing liabilities. On the contrary, in the process of rationalizing and enabling sound debt management of the states, the total size of the debt of poorer states should be prevented from undue rise by transferring more resources to them by way of grants until they become viable to manage higher debt burden.

8. Fiscal health of the state is an important factor at the macro level. It is evident from our analysis that political commitment to social sector has to extend beyond raising relative fiscal allocations. It has also to find resources to finance their sectors. The fiscal stress experienced in 1990's during the study period implies that enhancing allocations to social sector would require the structuring the state finance as well. However, the raising of allocations for social sectors as well as restructuring of state finance are easily possible when NSDP growth is more than growth in public debt and the rate of growth of population is controlled.
9. Lack of understanding and co-ordination of synergy among the programmes designed and implementation by the government for social sector and recognition of linkages between economic growth and human development on the one hand inhibits government from reallocating substantial proportion of budgetary resources away from productive sectors towards social sector. Therefore, there is a need to recognize and highlight the linkages between economic growth and social sectors on the hand and the role of social sectors is enhancing equity on the other.
10. Social infrastructure and maintenance which bears the burden cut in revenue expenditure may benefit from abolition of artificial distinction between plan and non plan expenditure. Rethinking on institutional role of the state planning bodies and central planning commission needs to be undertaken when allocations of resources are guided by markets. Transfer to states partly as as fixed sum and the rest linked to specific programme/project-with or without

incentive payment-can ameliorate the cascading effect of lower than anticipated revenue collection. There is need to break the nexus between state governments revenue deficit with that of the central government by making the committed expenditure on social infrastructure free from economic growth cycle. Incentive based transfer to sector specific and project specific is required to improve productivity of capital expenditure.

11. It is necessary to review the planning process and do away with the plan/non-plan dichotomy as the TFC urged. The integrity of the constitutional scheme of transfer s would require all revenue transfers to be mediated by FC. This would imply the plethora of centrally sponsored schemes would end and the plan grants also should come within the purview of the FC with the PC asked to look after only the capital requirement of the state which are deficient in infrastructures.

BIBLIOGRAPHY

Books:

1. Alessandro Prati, Stopping a run on government debt, Journal of Monetary Economics, Vol. No. 27, April 2 (1991)
2. Amalesh Banerjee & Biman Kar, Economic Planning and Development of Northeastern states Economic Reform and Response of states, Kanishka Publishers, New Delhi 1999
3. Anand, S. & Ravallion, M., "Human Development in Poor Countries: On the Role of Private Incomes and Public Services", Journal of Economic Perspectives, Vol. 7. No.1. 1993
4. A. Premchand, Government Financial Management: Issues and Country Studies IMF, Washington DC, 1990
5. A. Premchand, Ethical Dimensions of Public Expenditure Management, Economic Political Weekly, Vol xxxlx No. 8, Feb 21, 2004
6. Sengupta Arjun, LDC Problem Some Reflections on Proposed Solutions; Economic Political Weekly, April 29, 1989
7. B.A. Prakash, Keralas Economic Development issues and Problems, Sage Publications, 1999
8. Bhatia H.L. Public Finance, Vikas Publishing House Pvt. Ltd., 2000
9. Balbir Kaur & Sangita Misra, Social Sector Expenditure and Attainments: An Analysis of Indian States Reserve Bank of India; Occasional Papers Vol. 24, Nos. 1 and 2, Summer and Monsoon, 2003

10. Brian Pinto & Farah Zahir, Why Fiscal Adjustment Now Economic and Political Weekly Vol. No. 10, March 6, 2004

11. B. S. Sreekantaradhaya, Public Debt and Economic Development in India; Sterling Publishers Private Ltd. New Delhi, 1972

12. Cohen D., "Fiscal Sustainability and a Contingency Trust Fund" in Brixi H and Schick A (ed) Government at Risk: Contingent Liabilities and Fiscal Risk, The World Bank, Washington D.C. 2002

13. Datt Ruddar & K.P.M., Sundharam, Indian Economy, S. Chand & Co., New Delhi, 2005

14. David Alan Aschauer, Does public Capital Crowd out Private Capital, Journal of Monetary Economics, North Holland, 1989

15. Gopal Ji,Suman Bhakri, Human development in India Anne Books, New Delhi, 2004

16. Gupta R.K., Center-State Fiscal Relations under Indian Constitution; Deep and Deep Publications, New Delhi, 1992

17. Damudar Nepram, Centre-State Financial Relations, A study With reference to Manipur, Unpublished, Ph.D. thesis, Manipur University, 1998

18. D.M. Nanjundappa, Inter-Governmental Financial Relations in India, Sterling Publishers Private Limited, New Delhi, 1974

19. D. K. Mishra, Public debt and Economic Development in India, Print House, (India), Lucknow, 1984

20. Dietmar Wellisch, Theory of Public Finance in a Federal State, Cambridge University Press, 2000

21. Doss Veda, Impact of Planning on Centre-State Financial Relations in India, National Publishing House, New Delhi, 1978

22. Dreze, J. & Sen, A.K., "Hunger and Public Action" Oxford University Press, New York, 1989

23. G. Thimaiah, Federal Fiscal Systems of Australia and India; Associated Publishing House, New Delhi, 1976
24. G. Thimaiah, Burden of Union Loans on the States, Sterling Publishers Pvt. Ltd, New Delhi, 1977
25. G. Thimmaiah, Critique of the Finance Commission, Wheelar Publishing, New Delhi, 1981
26. G. Thimaiah & Hemlata Rao, Finance Commission and Centre-state and Financial Relations, Ashish Publishing House, New Delhi, 1986
27. Hicks Ursula K., Development Finance, Oxford University Press, London, 1965
28. Indira Rajaraman, A Study of Debt Sustainability at State and others level in India, RBI, 2005
29. IS Gulati, Centre-State Budgetary Transfers, Oxford University Press, 1987
30. Jhingal M. L. The Economics of Development and Planning, Konarak Publishers Pvt. Ltd, New Delhi, 2005
31. Janak Raj Puri, Fiscal Deficit of states in India, Atlantic Publishers and Distributor, 2001
32. K.S. Ramchandran, Drowned in Debt, Vices Publishing House Pvt. Ltd., 1990
33. Kiran Barman, India's Public Debt and Policy since Independence, Chugh Publications, Allahabad, 1978
34. K. Seeta Prabhu, Economic Reforms and Social Development: A study of two Indian States. (Strategies for Human Development in India-Volume 3, Sage Publications, New Delhi, 2001
35. Kothari C.R., Research Methodology and Techniques, Willy Eastern Pvt. Ltd. 4835/24, Ansari Rd., Daryaganj, New Delhi, 2005
36. K.N. Reddy & K.K. Tripathy, Priorities in resource Allocation for Health Care in India: A Basic needs Approach, Asian Economic Review, Vol. No. 2, Aug, 1991

37. Mugrave, Richard & Peggy B., A Public Finance in Theory and Practice, Mc Graw-Hill Book Company, 1989
38. P.N. Pimpley. et al, Social Development: Processes and Consequences, Department of Sociology Punjab University, Chandigarh, Rawat Publications, 1989
39. Prabhu, K. Seeta "Social sector Expenditure and Human Development: A study of Indian States, Development Research Group, Vol. No.6, RBI. Mumbai,1993
40. Ravindra Dholkia, Fiscal Sustainability of Debt of States—A study: IIM Ahmadabad, 2004
41. Rajendra Jain, State Finances in India, Progress Publishers, Bhopal, 1978
42. Rao, Hemlata Centre-State Financial Relations in India, Allied publishers Pvt. Ltd. New Delhi, 1981
43. Rajendra Jain, State Finances in India, Progress Publishers, Bhopal, 1978
44. Ruddar Datt, Human Development and Economic Development; Deep & Deep Publications Pvt. Ltd., New Delhi, 2005
45. Ruddar Datt (edited), Human Development and Economic Development; Deep and Deep publications Pvt. Ltd., Indian Economic Association, New Delhi, 2002
46. S.N. Lal, Problems of Public Borrowing in Underdeveloped Countries, Chugh Publications, Allahabad, 1978
47. Stephen Howes & Ashok Lahria and others, State-Level Reforms in India Towards Effective Government, MacMilan, New Delhi, 2003
48. Tapan Kumar Shandilya, Central Loans to States Under Five Year Plans, Deep & Deep Publications, New Delhi, 1991
49. Tyagi. B.P. Public Finance, Jai Prakash Nath & Co. Pvt. Ltd., Meerut U.P., 2000
50. Vithal B.P.R. & Sastry M.L., Fiscal Federalism in India, Oxford University Press, New Delhi, 2001
51. V. Kumar, Government Expenditure and Economic Development, Criterion Publications, New Delhi, 1986

Journals and Reports:

52. Amaresh Bagchi, Symposium on Report of Twelfth Finance Commission Introduction and Overview, Economic Political Weekly, July 30, 2005
53. A.World Bank Report State Fiscal Reforms in India, Progress and Prospects, Macmillan, First Publication, 2005
54. Ahluwalia M.S. "Economic Performance of States in Post Reforms Period" Economic and Political Weekly, 35(19) 2000
55. Abha Prasad, Rajan Goyal & Anupam Prakash, State's Debt and Debt Relief, Economic and Political Weekly, June 26, 2004
56. Rossman P.J., "A Political Theory of Intergovernmental Grants", Public Choice, Vol. No. 78, 1994
57. Indira Raja Raman & Debdatta Majumdar, Equity and Consistency Properties of TFC Recommendations, Economic and Political Weekly, July 30, 2005
58. Government of Manipur:

- Memorandum of Understanding entered into between Government of Manipur & Government of India on 20-06-2002 Finance Department, June (2002)
- White paper on Manipur State Finances Finance Department, June (2002)
- Finance Accounts 1972-73 to 2005-06
- Report of the Comptroller and Auditor General of India for the year ended 31 march 1992,1994,1995,2001,2002 and 2004
- Statistical Abstract of Manipur (various issues) Directorate of Economics and Statistics.
- Economic Survey (various issues) Directorate of Economics and Statistics
- Government of India-Economic survey (various issues)

- Memorandum of Understanding entered into between government of Manipur & Government of India on 20-06-2002 Finance department June (2002)
- White paper on Manipur State Finances Finance Department June (2002)
- Finance Accounts 1972-73 to 2005-06
- Report Of the Comptroller and Auditor General of India for the year ended 31 march 1992 1994 1995 2001 2002 2004
- Statistical Abstract of Manipur (various issues) Directorate of Economics and Statistics.
- Economic Survey (various issues) Directorate of Economics and Statistics
- Government of India-Economic survey(various issues)

59. G.R. Reddy, Twelfth Finance Commission and Backward States, Economic and Political Weekly, August 12, 2006
60. Kh. Jayantakumar Singh, Burden of Public Debt in Manipur, Journal of the NEC, Vol., 14,No. 3, July-Sept., 1994
62. K. Srinivasa Rao Expenditure pattern of Andhra Pradesh and its impact on Social and Human development, Yojana, February, 2003
63. Ministry of Finance, Indian Public Finance Statistics-2001-02 Government of India, 2002
64. Lane T.D. "Market Discipline" Staff Papers, International Monetary Fund, Vol. 40, 1993
65. N. J. Kurian Debt Relief for States, Economic and Political Weekly, July 30, 2005
66. Noel M. "Building Sub national Debt Markets in Developing and Transition Economies" Policy Research Working Paper 2339, The World Bank. 2000
67. Nirvikar Singh Inching Federal transfers towards maturity The Financial Express Kolkata, Thrusday March 24, 2005
68. Omkar Goswami Rethinking state Government debts, Telegraphs Monday June 14, 2004

69. NIPFP Trends and issues in Indian Federal Finance Allied Publishers Private Ltd., 1981

70. N. J. Kurian, A watershed for Centre-state Fiscal relations, The Financial Express, Kolkata, Saturday, March 12, 2005

71. Planning Commission National Human Development Report (2002)

72. Pinaki Charaborty: Debt Swap in a Interest Regime, Unequal Gains and Future Worries, Economic and Political Weekly, October 1, 2005.

73. Prasad A., Goyal R. & Prakash A., "States Debt and Debt Relief", Economic and Political Weekly, Vol., 39 No. 26, 2004

74. Reserve Bank of India (RBI):

- The Handbook Of Statistics on the Indian Economy
- Annual Reports (various issues)
- Bulletins (various issues)
- A Study of Budgets (various issues)
- Report on Currency and Finance
- Occasional Papers (various issues)

75. Report of the Working Group on Compilation of State Government Liabilities December 30, 2005, Dr. Rakesh Mohan Deputy Governor Reserve Bank of India, Mumbai

76. Report of the Advisory Committee on Ways and Means Advances to State Governments, reserve Bank of India, 2003.

77. Reserve Bank of India, Report of The Technical Committee on State Government Guarantees, 1999.

78. Rajendra R. Vaidya, Borrowing, Debt Management and Contingent Liabilities: A Study of Indian State Govt. This report was prepared by consultants for The Asian Development Bank (2005)

79. Ravindra H. Dholkia, Regional Disparity in Economic and Human developmemt in India Economic Political Weekly Sept 27, 2003

80. Ravindra H. Dholkia, Measurement issues in comparing Fiscal performance of states, Economic Political Weekly, March 8, 2003

81. Rao, M.G., "State Finances in India: Issues and Challenges" Economic and Political Weekly, Vol. 37 No.32, 2002

82. Rao M.G., "Invisible Transfers in Indian Federalism" Public Finance, Vol. 52 No. (3-4) 1997

83. Government of India Report of the Eleventh Finance Commission Akalank Publication, New Delhi, 2000

84. Government of India Report of the Twelfth Financc Commission [2005-10] November, 2004.

85. S Gurumuthi, Twelfth finance Commission and States' debt Burden; Economic and Political Weekly, Oct. 5, 2002

86. Summary and Research on Fiscal Federalism in India (1991)

87. S. Rao Aiyagari & Ellen R. McGrattan, The optimum quantity of Debt Journal of Monetary Economics 42 (1988)

88. S. Mahendra Dev & Jos Mooji, Social Sector Expenditure in the 1990s Analysis of Central and State Budgets, Economic Political Weekly, March 2, 2002

89. Shah, A. "Fiscal Decentralization in Developing and Transition Economies: Progress, Problems and Promise" Policy Research Working Paper no. 3282, World Bank, (2004) Washington D.C.

90. Shankar Acharya, "India's Macroeconomic Management in the 1990s", Economic and Political Weekly, (2002) Vol. 37 no.16.

91. Singh N. and G. Vashishtha, Patterns in Center-State Fiscal Transfers: An Illustrative Analysis, The Economic and Political Weekly (2004), Nov. 6

92. Tapas Kumar, Sen Public Expenditure on Human Development in India: Trends and issues Feb. 1992, No. 16
93. Ter-Minassian T. eds., Fiscal Federalism in Theory and Practice International Monetary Fund, Washington (1997)
94. The Sarkaria Commission "Report on Centre-State Relations", Government of India, New Delhi, 1988
95. V. Sridhar Finance commission: Short-changing the states Frontline April 8, 2005
96. Vincezo Denicolo & Massimo Matteuzi, Public Debt and the Pasinetti Paradox, Cambridge Journal Economics, 1990.
97. World Bank State Fiscal Reforms in India: Progress and Prospects, Macmillan India Ltd. (2005) Delhi
98. Webb S.B., "Fiscal responsibility Laws for Subnational Discipline: The Latin American Experience", World Bank Working Paper no. 309, (2004) Washington D.C.
99. World Bank World Development Indicators. (2003)